Browsing in the
BRENDONS

Sheila Eckhart

REDCLIFFE PRESS

First published in 1995 by Redcliffe Press

A CIP Record for this book is available from the British Library

REDCLIFFE PRESS
Halsgrove House
Lower Moor Way
Tiverton Devon EX16 6SS
Telephone 01884 243242
Facsimile 01884 243325

ISBN 1 872971 19 9

Printed in England by Longdunn Press Ltd, Bristol.

Contents

Introduction

This book is about a small range of hills called the Brendons. It is not a tourist guide or an historical document, but one person's thoughts and findings in beautiful countryside. The Brendons are in the Exmoor National Park and the area I have chosen is within the perimeters of the A358, A39, A396 and B3227 roads.

Another man-made boundary also marks the border roughly between the Brendons and the Quantocks – the West Somerset Railway, which runs from Bishops Lydeard to Williton and then on to Minehead. This old steam railway with its reminder of bygone times, follows the A358 from Taunton to Williton, both running more or less side by side along the foot of the Brendons on the eastern side. I will be taking in Watchet and the coastline as far as Dunster, then back to Wheddon Cross on the A396, and finally winding down to Exebridge, Bampton and Wiveliscombe on the B3227.

The book is divided into four chapters, and a look at the Ordnance Survey map will show why. It may seem that too much time is spent talking about the churches, but they are the oldest buildings in our land and certain features and characteristics are chosen which are peculiar only to a particular church. From the thirteenth to the fifteenth centuries the county became very wealthy through the wool trade; even today we sometimes call churches of that period wool churches. Many were rebuilt of stone at that time, previously having been small wooden structures. The dead were shrouded in wool in support of the wool trade. In 1538 Thomas Cromwell, Henry VIII's Chief Minister, ordered the keeping of church registers, but not all registers date from that time.

The pre-Reformation church was one of spectacle and great ritual; it was elaborately decorated with statues, stained glass windows, screens and bosses. However at the time of the Reformation, fanatics of various creeds mutilated many of these articles. Suddenly the new religion was forced upon everyone and even small villages in remote places like the Brendons felt the repercussions. They no longer had the Pope as head of the church, but the King. Some vicars refused to accept this and were executed. Church furnishings in some places were hidden away under a floor or in a barn; some of these are now returned to their proper places. Much the same thing happened during the Civil War. Clergymen were banished from their churches and zealous Puritans smashed and destroyed crosses, statues and the like.

With the restoration of the monarchy in 1660 the church again became a place of meeting and prayer. By the time Victoria came to the throne most churches were once more in a great state of dilapidation and a strong religious revival took place. The country again became wealthy with the progress of the Industrial Revolution and the churches underwent drastic restoration. Unfortunately many more medieval objects were destroyed. The church is a place where much history of the parish can be found. Regrettably these days we have vandals of a different nature and so churches whose policy has always been to stay open from sunrise to sunset may now be found locked, although there is usually someone living nearby from whom a key may be obtained.

> Whenever I see a Church,
> I pay a little visit,
> So when at last I am carried in,
> The Lord won't say 'Who is it'?

There are also many ancient houses in this area such as Dunster Castle, Gaulden Manor, Combe Sydenham, Orchard Wyndham and Bardon House to mention a few. These are true monuments to our past and should be cherished.

However well we might think we know our own county there are always many more exciting things to find. At the start I knew nothing of the folklore or history of the Brendons except that there had been a mineral railway. I liked the diversity of the Brendons from the moorland to the forests and the forests down into the valleys; the spectacular views of the sea stretching across the Channel to Wales, the deep glens and combes all luxuriantly watered; the patchwork of green fields filled sometimes with fluffy white woolly sheep or black and white cows; the small villages dotted about. This small area of hill country is studded with places of interest, footpaths and wildlife. Where else in the world could one find such variety, beauty and peace?

The valleys and combes were cut over thousands of years by the flow of the streams and the rivers following torrential rain and storms.
In the springtime moorland, such as Haddon Hill, is scattered with golden flowering gorse and the fresh green of the young bracken, which dies to a dull brown by autumn. Whortleberries and bell heather give a purple hue. Then there are the ploughed fields with the deep red soil which is always a surprise to the stranger, the same colour as the sandstone which is used for many Brendon buildings.

Prehistoric man scratched a living on these hills making tracks which ran from one hilltop to another. We still use these tracks today. Some have widened into roads to meet the needs of modern traffic, others remain footpaths. After the feet of man and the cantering hooves, carriages and then farming development all made their mark. To-day a delicate balance between the farming community and conservation is being attempted.

Standing on the moorland at the top of Grabbist Hill at Dunster in 1848, Mrs Alexander was so enthralled with the surroundings that she composed the hymn which we all know so well to-day – *All things bright and beautiful*.

On 9 March 1891 there started the biggest snow-fall for many years, certainly within living memory, and some snow drifts in the hills around Taunton were recorded as being up to 20 feet deep, blocking most roads. A few villages were cut off for as long as six weeks.

Two World Wars made little impact on the Brendons compared with the rest of the country. Nevertheless in the Second World War each large village had its Home Guard originally called Local Defence Volunteers, or LDVs. The inhabitants probably didn't

6

suffer from the food rationing introduced in January 1940, as much as the large cities. Being a farming area they were practically self sufficient. All spare ground had to be ploughed up to grow vegetables. Have you ever tasted rabbit stew? Rabbits were very plentiful. Ordinary families who were not farmers kept a few chickens in their back yards and so had free range eggs and a bird for Christmas. During the Second World War, American soldiers were camped on the Brendons waiting for the word which would despatch them to an unknown destination. It turned out to be the Normandy beaches.

In every village there is a memorial to the two World Wars. Sometimes the same surname is mentioned two or three times, probably meaning that brothers or father and son were killed.

A 92 year old farmer way up in the hills was asked by a tourist,
'To what do you owe your long life?'
'To being born so long ago', he replied.

The Brendons are famous for their beech hedges; some are quite high and in places the trees have grown tall and the tops meet one another, forming an amazing green tunnel. There is a lot of heathland and afforested areas and these attract siskins and nightjars. The nightjars come out at dusk and it is wonderful just to sit in the deepening twilight amongst the bracken and listen to the churring of their courtship. The buzzard population on these hills is also large.

Situated between the Quantocks and Exmoor, the Brendons are also a home of the red deer, Britain's largest wild animal. These animals have only one enemy – man. They live on vegetation and hide mainly in the woodland.

There are also roe deer, fallow deer, foxes, badgers, otters, squirrels, bats and many more animals.

Exmoor, which includes part of the Brendons, was designated as a National Park in 1954. Most of the Brendons consists of private farmland but there are many footpaths. Under close control and regularly wormed, dogs are also welcome.

I will ask the reader a question. How wide is a footpath? The answer is at the end of the Introduction so that there is time to think. I would walk as many footpaths as possible on these hills.

Some farmers keep footpaths clear and mark the way very well; unfortunately there are a few who make it very difficult by locking gates, putting up electric fences etc. Most walkers these days are knowledgeable about the countryside; they do shut gates and walk around the edges of fields. Farmers who clearly mark the footpaths are therefore wise because at least they don't have ramblers wandering all over their farms looking for the correct way.

Many public houses came to my notice because of their part in history. They nearly all serve very good food; I cannot mention them all, but in this area of Somerset and Devon they cater very well for the tourist. I ate in many of them on my travels and I did not find a bad one. There is a cross-roads high up on the hills near Beulah Chapel, this is the boundary of Old

Cleeve parish and is marked by a large stone called 'The Naked Boy' or sometimes 'Four Naked Boys' or even the 'Devil Stone' as it is supposed to hold the Devil. Legend says there was a boy who was a drunkard associated with this junction. Suicides and witches were buried at cross roads so there may be some truth in The Naked Boy.

The Brendon Hills are particularly noted for their Halloween Nights and the making of lanterns from swedes and turnips, which would have candles placed inside to shine through the eyes and mouth. The lanterns were usually set outside houses as decorations. Although this ritual also takes place in other parts of the country, it is thought probably to have started around the Brendons. In some areas they call it 'Punky Night'. Also on Halloween night it is believed that the images of all the people who will die during the following year pass through the churchyards.

The Bristol Channel on the northern edge of the Brendons has exceptionally large tides which means that when the tide goes out a very large expanse of sand, silt and mud is uncovered on the seaside beaches. On the high cliffs between Porlock and Lynmouth, there is about a fifty-foot difference between the high and low tide marks.

Now, a piece of advice for walkers. Everyone occasionally gets blisters. The idea is to gather sheep's wool on the walk, take it home, wash it and tease it out to get all the bits out of it. It can then be worn as a pad inside socks or on any tender area. I have tried it and it works.

The answer to my question about a footpath: the width of a footpath is six feet, that is, the width of a coffin and four bearers. Remember these footpaths were used by all before any means of transport became available and often run from an ancient village or farmstead to a church.

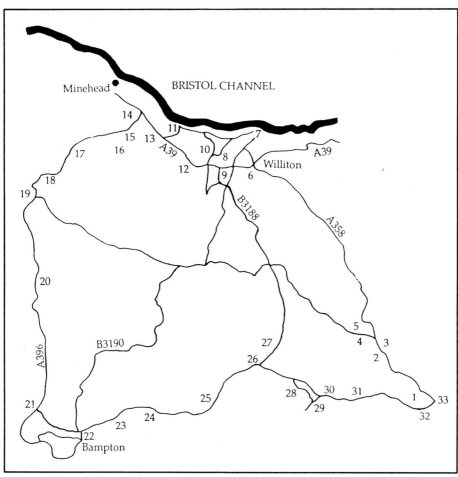

1. Norton Manor Camp
2. Bishops Lydeard Station
3. Cedar Falls
4. Sandhill Park Hospital
5. Combe Florey
6. Williton
7. Watchet
8. Washford
9. Cleeve Abbey
10. Old Cleeve
11. Blue Anchor
12. Bilbrook
13. Carhampton
14. Dunster
15. Gallox Hill Fort
16. Bats Castle
17. Timberscombe
18. Cutcombe
19. Wheddon Cross
20. Bridgetown
21. Exebridge
22. Bampton
23. Shillingford
24. Petton Cross
25. Waterrow
26. Wiveliscombe
27. Ford
28. Quaking House
29. Milverton
30. Preston Bowyer
31. Hillcommon
32. Norton Fitzwarren
33. Cross Keys

NORTON MANOR CAMP – Within this Ministry of Defence property, surrounded by barbed wire, with security systems and soldiers on guard, lies a lovely old manor house. It was built in 1842 at the cost of £20,000, by Charles Noel Welman, on the south side of Knowle Hill overlooking his land. His family crest adorns the front of the building in two places, and it is also represented on the ceiling over the main staircase. The house has changed hands six times since the Welmans were in residence; one of the owners was Francis Bowes Lyon (the Queen Mother's uncle) who bought the house in 1909 for the sum of £29,000. He owned it for only two years.

In 1939, with the onset of the Second World War, a compulsory purchase order acquired the property for the War Department, and the 22nd Searchlight Militia department RA TA unit moved in. The Americans arrived in 1943, and built an evacuation hospital in the grounds from wooden buildings despatched from Canada in sections and then re-erected here in blocks. The basic layout of the covered walkways remains to this day. Around the same time, Musgrove Park Hospital in Taunton was built in the same manner. In 1946, the camp reverted to the British Army and was taken over by the Army Apprentices School for four years. It then went to various Regiments until in May 1983, a small advance party from 40 Commando Royal Marines took over from the junior soldiers. The camp was refurbished and improved for the full arrival of 40 Commando in August 1983. These men saw action in Northern Ireland, the Falklands and Kuwait.

There is the inevitable ghost story here. At the turn of the century a young maid was in her room under the roof, when she somehow got into a wooden box seat under her bedroom window. The seat must have locked and she couldn't get out. By the time she was found to be missing she had starved to death. She now haunts the manor house. Just recently, one of the cleaners was cleaning the bathroom on the same floor and as she turned around, this young girl was standing in the doorway. One of the camp's padres would not sleep in that room. I was taken to see the window seat and the room was occupied by a soldier. Obviously he is not superstitious.

BISHOPS LYDEARD STATION – This station, along with part of the village, is set within our triangle of the Brendon Hills but the main village of Bishops Lydeard, including the church, is on the other side of the road.

A group of local landowners put forward a proposal in 1856 for a railway line to run from Taunton to Watchet. They called it the West Somerset Railway. Being business men they probably saw the potential of trucking iron ore from Watchet as the Mineral Railway was already shipping iron ore and slate down to Watchet. On 17 August, 1857 an Act of Parliament was passed to allow the West Somerset Railway to lay a track joining the B.& E.R. (Bristol & Exeter) junction at Norton Fitzwarren. Brunel was put in charge of this operation but he died in 1859 before the line was constructed. On 31 March, 1862 this broad gauge rail link was opened. The first passenger service from Watchet ran at 8.45 that morning. In 1871 there was a further Act to extend the line to Minehead and this section opened on 16 July, 1874, run by B.& E.R. Both sections were converted to standard gauge in October 1882. The whole length of railway was taken over by the G.W.R. in 1897, but the W.S.R. remained in name until 1922. The line was nationalised on 1 January, 1948 and became part of British Rail. In Beeching's report *The Reshaping of British Railways* in the early 1960s, this line came under the Beeching axe. The track remained and was taken over by a new company of mainly volunteers and enthusiasts. After much hard work it re-opened on 28 March, 1976 and named the West Somerset Railway once more. It ran from

The West Somerset Railway first ran in 1862, was closed under the
Beeching cuts in the 1960s and re-opened by enthusiasts in 1976.

Blue Anchor to Minehead. By June 1979, it was in operation all the way to Bishops Lydeard. It is the longest privately owned railway line in the country.

CEDAR FALLS — Further along the road lies Cedar Falls. Although not in the Brendons, it has an interesting history. This mansion house was originally built in the 1700s as Watts House. In 1902 it was purchased by the Boles family who were known for throwing lavish parties, with notable guests such as Lord Baden-Powell and Sir Winston Churchill. For a while during the war years Connaught House, a boys' boarding school at Weymouth, moved into Watts House. With its large grounds the school became mainly self sufficient. Cedar Falls was opened as a health farm in 1982 and has now become one of the country's leading establishments in that field.

SANDHILL PARK — This house was built in 1720 and enlarged in 1815. It has a large porch with eight Tuscan columns and it overlooks beautiful extensive grounds, the drive winding between magnificent trees. It was the home of the Lethbridge family, Lords of this vast Manor. In 1875 the Lord of the Manor was Sir Wroth Acland Lethbridge, by 1914 it had passed to Sir Wroth Christopher Lethbridge and Mrs Savill-Onley but a decade later one of the principal landowners was Somerset County Council.

During the Second World War the house was leased to the American 185th General Military Hospital. In their free time the soldiers used to troop off to the local public house at Bishops Lydeard, their excursion becoming known as the whisky trail. There was a small chapel within the grounds, known as The Chapel of Jesus.

After the war the house became a hospital mainly for disturbed and handicapped children. It was sold in 1991 for over a million pounds.

COMBE FLOREY – A delightful sleepy, picturesque village. First Lords of the Manor were the Cumbe family. At the time of Henry I, Baldwin de Cumbe held the Manor of the Bishop of Winchester; he was succeeded by Hugh de Flury. That was when the Manor took on its extra name.

A Sir John de Meriet who lived here in the thirteenth century had a wife, Maud who left John to become a nun at Cannington. When she died her husband wanted her brought back so that she could be buried with him. His request was refused by the church, but he managed to acquire her heart. This resulted in excommunication from the church and he was only pardoned when he returned the heart to Cannington.

The gatehouse is Elizabethan. It was originally four storeyed. A ghost of a lady is said to stand at a downstairs window looking up the road as if waiting for someone to return. She wears one of the large head-dresses common in Elizabethan times and before.

Combe Florey House is a large Devonian stone building built in 1675 but there was a house previous to this.

Sydney Smith, a poet and jester, became a canon of St Paul's Cathedral. He loved the country and he kept his house in the village after obtaining the post in London. One day he invited his friends down from London. These friends had heard of red deer living on the Quantocks and, loving to play tricks, Sydney Smith attached antlers to his donkeys and said they were red deer.

The well-loved authors Evelyn and Auberon Waugh made their home there. Evelyn used

The Elizabethan gatehouse of Combe Florey.

an ear trumpet and one day after he had dined at Orchard Wyndham he left this aid behind. He never collected it and it is now on show with other famous antiques at Orchard Wyndham.

There is a lovely riverside walk from the village to The Farmer's Arms. This thirteenth century thatched pub has its motto on the inn sign 'In God is our Trust'.

The village had a station on the West Somerset line. The milepost there reads 170/1, which means it is 170 miles from Paddington, and that piece of track is in the first quarter of a mile. There are signposts every quarter of a mile numbered this way from mainline London stations, so that when linesmen were told to mend a certain stretch of track they know exactly where to go. One may argue that London is not quite that far, but this track is measured via Bristol and Swindon.

In 1848 a National School was erected for boys and girls.

Jack White, a farmer from Stogumber, lived in the village. He was one of Somerset's best bowlers and he became a cricket legend when he played for England against Australia in 1928-29. In the fourth test match he bowled an incredible 124 overs, taking 13 wickets for 256 runs. It was during a heat wave and he had continually to change his shirt and have cold drinks. The big black gates of the Somerset cricket ground were given by him and bear his initials.

The church at Combe Florey.

This is where I heard a cricket joke:

A keen cricketer met Saint Peter. 'Tell me,' he asked, 'Are there any cricket pitches in heaven?'
'Do you want the good news or the bad news?' asked Saint Peter.
'The good news please,' said the cricketer.
'Well, there are wonderful cricket grounds in heaven, much better than here on earth.'
'Thank you, then what is the bad news?' asked the cricketer.
'You are batting next Wednesday,' replied Saint Peter.

A war memorial in the churchyard was erected by the villagers in 1920 in remembrance of 45 men from the village lost in the Great War. It can be imagined what that meant to a village of this size; that number would have been nearly one generation of youths.

Driving past the church and taking the little lane on the right, one soon comes to a folly on the right hand side. This tall square building, looking across to the Quantock Hills, was built by a farmer called John Winter and was known as 'The Winter

A noted Somerset folly: the Winter Tower, named after the local farmer who built it.

Tower'. It is now being converted into a smart private residence. (See Ash Priors).

THE CHURCH OF ST PETER AND ST PAUL – The perpendicular church is dated 1292 but there would have been an earlier church on this site. Indeed the font probably comes from it. On the floor in the north aisle of the church are the effigy tombs of Sir John de Meriet with his two wives. His first wife, Mary de Mohun, died aged eighteen years; his second wife, Elizabeth Paynel, died in 1344. Sir John has his legs crossed, but no one knows why, as he didn't go to the Crusades. John died in 1327.

On the wall near these effigies is the place where the heart of Maud, the Cannington nun, was buried for a short time.

In the north aisle by the font is a brass plaque to Nicholas Fraunceis dated 1526. There is an even older Fraunceis tomb behind the organ dated 1485. The Fraunceis family were there for over four hundred years.

There is a Victorian east window in memory of Sydney Smith.

The church was restored in 1901.

A carved oak chancel screen was erected by his friends to the memory of Lieutenant Hyland, killed in the Great War.

The screen was then extended across the aisle in memory of other parishioners who also fell in the war.

WILLITON – This town is not in the Brendons, but it comes within my triangle. To the east lie the Quantock Hills and to the south west, the Brendons and Exmoor. There was a settlement here in the Bronze Age and it is known that the Saxons invaded in the fifth century.

North of Williton the road divides into two but both roads lead to Watchet. By the left hand fork, opposite Williton School, is a field of rough common land where in AD 918, the Saxons slaughtered all the invading Danes not quick enough to get back to their ships. To this day the field and battle are called 'Battlegore'. There are large mounds, known collectively as Grabburrows, which are the burial places of those Danes. Bones have been found at the site.

The Methodists preached here from 1790, but in 1806 John and Mary Stoate allowed the services to be conducted in their home until a chapel was acquired in 1820. In 1883 a larger building, together with school room and minister's house, was built at a cost of £4500. A plaque in the chapel tells of the devotion of John and Mary.

There are some old thatched cottages by the church and Townsend House was built as the workhouse; it dates from 1830.

An item from the *Free Press* of 27 March, 1915 reads as follows:

> Coffins for the Williton Workhouse were 30 shillings each. The Board of Guardians also accepted tenders for other supplies as follows; unskimmed milk 2¹/d. per quart; soap 3¹/d. per lb; tobacco 4s. 10d. per lb; scrubbing brushes 9s. 6d. per dozen; calico 5d. per yard; men's coloured handkerchiefs 1s. 6¹/d. per dozen; men's suits £1 5s. 0d. each; beef for the inmates 7¹/d. per pound; slightly dearer for officers.

In 1915 £40 was allowed by the Williton Parish Council for street lighting.

Williton became a town in the nineteenth century when the turnpike trusts came together for the benefit of the whole of West Somerset. On the Taunton road can be found Toll Cottage. There is a story that a local candlemaker carried his goat out to the pasture every day through back lanes and gardens instead of leading it up the road, to avoid having to pay at the tollgate.

The road which runs from here to Minehead is the main road from Bridgwater and Taunton. A new bypass was promised in 1939, but to date there is no sign of it. With increasing traffic along this road the three villages which span it – namely Carhampton, Bilbrook and Washford – suffer greatly from pollution and accidents.

There is now a new long-awaited fire station, officially opened in January 1993, at a cost of £220,000. Before the Second World War the fire station consisted of only a hand pump. A new station was built in Killick Way in 1940 at a cost of £50 and in 1961 it was upgraded to a two-pump station after the closure of Watchet Fire Station.

The West Somerset Railway station is quite interesting, with shop and coffee place; platform tickets can be obtained to have a look around. The milepost here reads 178/1.

A museum at Orchard Mill dates back to the days when the mill was in full operation, with the machinery and mill stones, built in 1616, still intact. There is also a gift shop and a tea room where Somerset cream teas are sold; or they can be eaten in the garden alongside the mill wheel. A licensed restaurant serves wholesome home cooked meals.

One local pub is called The Wyndham Arms taking its name from the famous local family; ask inside about the ghost. Another lovely eating house here is The Mason's Arms, formerly a beer shop. It occupied the former Shutgate toll house. The Egremont Hotel, named after the Lords of the Manor, the Wyndhams, Earls of Egremont, opened about 1861 for the growing trade caused by the new turnpike road. The title of Earl of Egremont became extinct in 1854.

Orchard Wyndham House is a large private manor house. Thomas de Orchard built the first house here in 1287. The Pophams held the manor from 1420 when a sole heiress, Joan, married Richard Popham of Alfoxton. Their only daughter, also named Joan, married John Sydenham of Combe Sydenham in 1448. It remained in the hands of the Sydenhams for eighty years but it has been the home of the Wyndhams since 1522, when Elizabeth Sydenham married John Wyndham of Norfolk. Generations later Francis Wyndham, after holding Dunster Castle in the Civil War, helped King Charles II to escape to France after the battle of Worcester in 1651.

Sir William Wyndham was implicated in the English Jacobites' rebellion in 1715; when it was discovered that he had Jacobite leanings, he escaped to Orchard Wyndham. He was found by the Army but managed to escape. Making an excuse to say goodbye to his wife, he jumped out of an upstairs window straight onto the back of his horse. He rode to friends at Blackdown who hid him until he disguised himself as a priest and escaped to France. Eventually, Sir William returned to England and gave himself up. He was then imprisoned in the Tower of London but freed after the Scottish uprising had failed.

A William Wyndham was MP for Taunton in 1660 and 1661, and a Sir Charles Wyndham was MP for Taunton in 1747 when he was called to the Upper House.

In the 1980s Orchard Wyndham was the scene of a robbery. Doctor Katherine Wyndham actually climbed down the drainpipe on the same side of the house as her ancestor had done to raise the alarm, but there was no horse.

Since the Orchards built the centre of the house in the thirteenth century, successive generations of Sydenhams and Wyndhams have added and enhanced the building to suit their needs. It is a homely house still lived in by the present generation of Wyndhams. They are trying to restore the fabric of the building, and the surrounding woodlands and gardens, with the help of English Heritage. It is a private house not generally open to the public, except on special occasions or by arrangement.

ST PETER'S CHURCH – The church was restored in 1858, when the north aisle was built. There is an alabaster font in the church dated 1666. The cliffs around Watchet and Blue Anchor are formed of alabaster, which was quarried in medieval times. This is a rather soft pink and white stone.

In 1170 Reginald Fitzurse, who held the manor of Williton, was one of the four knights responsible for the murder of Thomas à Becket. Facing banishment for his crime, he handed half the manor over to his brother, Robert on condition that he built a chapel of ease. Today Williton's church of St Peter has grown on the foundations of this chapel.

THOMAS À BECKET – It was Henry II who appointed Thomas à Becket as Archbishop of Canterbury. Thomas was his friend and Henry thought that he would now be able to bring the church under his own authority. But Thomas sided with the church and Henry was furious. It is said that one night sitting around a table with his knights discussing national affairs, Henry said 'Will no-one rid me of this turbulent priest?' Four of the knights took him at his word and on 29 December, 1170, Richard Brito, Hugh de Moreville, Reginald Fitzurse and William de Tracy confronted Thomas à Becket. Thomas had just returned from six years in exile and his friend Henry II was now his bitterest foe. The knights seized the Archbishop and he tried to shake them off, throwing Fitzurse to the ground. Tracy then shouted 'Strike, strike', and Brito's sword sank deep into Thomas's head. He was murdered on the altar steps of Canterbury Cathedral. He was buried in the crypt and two days later a series of miracles began. Thomas was canonised in 1173 by Pope Alexander III. The famous hospital of St Thomas near the Houses of Parliament in London was named after this Archbishop.

WATCHET – Over one thousand years ago when King Alfred of Wessex was fighting the Danes, they invaded this coastline many times, actually coming ashore here in AD 987 and AD 988. Ever since that time Watchet has been a busy little trading port. The Vikings streamed inland pillaging and plundering as they went. They burnt down the settlements of Watchet and Williton.

In AD 978 a Royal Mint was founded by Aethelred II and it continued to produce coins

West Docks, Watchet: rail trucks of iron ore were tipped direct into the waiting ships below.

until after the reign of Stephen, turning out silver pennies. Some of these were used as 'danegeld'. Quite a number have survived and are in museums in Stockholm and Copenhagen.

In medieval times Watchet became a borough.

In the sixteenth century the port was one of the busiest on the Severn Sea, as the Bristol Channel was then called. It carried cargoes such as coal, salt and Welsh sheep.

In 1608 Thomas Salkeld – a notorious pirate – took over Lundy Island with his gang of outlaws. They led a reign of terror in the Bristol Channel, pillaging, murdering crews, sinking ships and making the seaway a very dangerous place. George Eskott, a Watchet sailor decided to lead a revolt against Salkeld; he planned the operation with a few fellow seamen and when they had overpowered the pirates they brought them to justice on the mainland. For this good deed George Eskott received a pension for life from a very grateful King James I.

In 1650 the ducking stool was in constant use by the Court Leet to punish 'Ye witches and scolds'. The Court Leet can still be seen at the rear of the Museum.

The Washford river supplies the paper mill and then runs into the harbour, walled in to avoid flooding.

During the eighteenth century Sir William Wyndham, Lord of the Manor and owner of the port, secured the passage of an Act of Parliament to build a more substantial harbour. It did not improve matters much and over the next century trade was very poor. Luckily for Watchet the iron ore industry started to expand, and in 1853 the Ebbw Vale Company secured the rights to operate the mines in the Brendon Hills. Spasmodically since the Roman period the mines had been privately worked. The port was chosen by the Welsh company to ship iron ore and slate across to Wales and the mineral railway was built. The siding ran alongside the West Pier and the trucks of ore were emptied straight into the ships below. Horses were used for shunting the trucks along the pier.

Small sailing ships often found it almost impossible to obtain insurance cover. In April 1884 the local shipowners held a meeting and decided to form their own insurance club. The Watchet Shipowners' Mutual Assurance Association also covered ships from nearby ports. Each member paid 3% of the value of his ship. Should a ship be lost the existing members would pay an additional levy of 3% of the already agreed value of the ship lost.

*The former gaol at Watchet,
at the rear of the museum.*

The simple system worked well until the disastrous gale of 28 December, 1900 when the harbour and most of its ships were destroyed.

A lifeboat was regularly launched from Watchet harbour from 1875 until 1944.

Good sea fishing can be had from this port; nearby Steart Flats are very productive with catches of dabs, rays and flounders. Dog-fish and conger eels can be caught by shore fishing from Dunster Beach.

Another Watchet character was John Short. Born in 1839, he wrote over 50 shanties. In 1864 his ship, *Levant*, ran the blockade of the American Civil War. He carried on singing until he died in 1933, aged 94.

The Market House is an early Victorian building. It now houses the Museum, where there is much information about the area and an interesting video presentation. It is well worth a visit and is certainly value for money.

The tall chimney of the paper mill founded almost three centuries ago can be picked out; The first paper was made by hand and the first paper making machine was introduced in 1869 by Mr A.C. Wansborough. As the paper mill progressed so did the dock, bringing in cargoes of wood pulp and esparto grass used in paper production. In 1898 there was a disastrous fire, after which the Wansborough mill went into the hands of the receivers. In 1901 it was bought by Mr W.H.Reed and from then on expanded. In 1977 the company changed hands again to the St Regis Group of New York.

In the mid and late twentieth century, the harbour not only handled imports associated with the paper mill, but also packaged timber. Exports were scrap and a regular freight to Portugal. The latter were mainly organised by a South Wales shipping agent whose business failed and shipments ceased in 1993. Future plans hope to set up a marina in the harbour which will boost the economy of the town and reverse the industrial decline.

The Baptist church's beginnings here were with the Countess of Huntingdon's Connection in 1766. A Baptist chapel was built in 1808. In 1992 work started to convert the former St Decuman's School into a new church. An appeal had been launched in 1988 and enough money was raised from the sale of the former chapels in Stogumber and Watchet to purchase the redundant school. There is a Methodist chapel by the station. The West Somerset Railway now puffs in and out of Watchet.

Kentsford House, largely rebuilt in 1600, and Orchard Wyndham were the homes of the Wyndham family. Florence Wyndham lived at Kentsford. One day she fell seriously ill, and thinking that she was dead, was interred in the family vault at St Decuman's. That night the sexton, having seen Florence's expensive rings, broke into the vault. When he tried to remove the rings he cut her skin, the fingers bled and the corpse started moving. The sexton ran from the vault terrified. Florence went home to her somewhat surprised husband.

Kentsford Bridge is an old two arched packhorse bridge.

The Holy Well, in a beautiful garden, lies down a steep little lane at the side of the church. The water which springs out of the hillside is covered by a small stone shelter, from where it runs into three basins. The spring never dries up even in long spells of very hot weather. Tradition has it that one should flip a coin into the water and wish, or have a quick sip as the water allegedly has medicinal properties. The Holy Well is reputed to be the place where Saint Decuman, a monk and hermit, lived. He is also reported to have returned here and washed his head after it had been cut off by a pagan. He became the patron saint of Watchet, Llandegyman in Wales and Degibma in Cornwall.

There is supposed to be a pack of wild hounds on Cleeve Hill. These are the Yeth Hounds and should anyone ever see these beasts it is a sign that the devil is coming to collect one of his own.

On Saturday 18 September, 1993 a new cemetery was opened by Doctor Katherine Wyndham. The land was given by the Wyndham estate as the cemetery around St Decuman's church was full. There was a tribute to members of the public who had donated over £2000 towards trees and rose bushes to plant around the cemetery. The contributions were in memory of 160 loved ones whose names were read out at the opening ceremony.

ST DECUMAN'S CHURCH — The church stands on a hill on the edge of town and was named after the holy man who sailed across the water from Wales on a raft made of reeds. There is a statue of St Decuman in a niche in the tower.

The thirteenth-century tiles on the chancel floor are believed to have been made at Cleeve Abbey. In the Wyndham Chapel (or North Chapel) a monument to Sir John Wyndham dates from 1574. Against the wall there are four-foot brass figures of John Wyndham dated 1572, with his wife, the Florence mentioned above, dated 1596.

On the chancel floor are two more interesting Wyndham tombs. One is to Edmund Wyndham who died in 1616. He was married to Margaret Chamberlayne and they had seven sons and one daughter. At least three of their sons, Edmund, Hugh and Francis, fought in the Civil War in 1645.

In 1970 the church was cleaned and redecorated by over 100 parishioners working voluntarily.

According to R.D.Blackmore, Lorna Doone's mother was buried in the churchyard.

There is a window which is perhaps outstanding throughout the country. It was presented by Richard Coeur de Lion after the Crusades. It had a wall built on each side of it, to save it from destruction by Cromwell.

THE CIVIL WAR — In 1642 Thomas Luttrell handed over Dunster Castle to the charge of Colonel Francis Wyndham for the Royalists. In 1643 Edmund Wyndham became High Sheriff of Somerset and the following year was given full command when Taunton was held by Colonel Robert Blake. On 14 December, Taunton was relieved by the Parliamentarians. It was a miracle that Blake had held out. Francis Wyndham still held out at Dunster Castle and Blake moved in to besiege Dunster, but at first his efforts were futile.

The Wyndham monument, St Decuman's Church, Watchet.

Soon Exeter fell to Fairfax; there was no hope for Francis Wyndham and on the 20 April, 1646 he surrendered. After the war Edmund Wyndham was exiled; he went to Boulogne and became Charles II's agent.

WASHFORD – This village sits astride the busy A39. There is a small railway museum.

The Tropiquaria is a must for all the family with animals, reptiles, plants and gardens in 12 acres of land on the site of the former radio station, built in 1933. Hot air from the BBC transmitters provides tropical temperatures for this indoor rain forest. There is an array of exotic and colourful fish and one can see coral reefs, meet a python, or wander into the jungle and find toads, tree frogs and much, much more.

St Pancras chapel has now been converted to a private residence.

The Washford Inn is a good refreshment stop.

In the centre of the village the old railway bridge once spanned the old Mineral Railway line.

The monks' path which runs to Old Cleeve Church is well worth walking. Along the path are the remains of an ancient cross.

I also walked down Stream Lane one August and the fields were blue with the small delicate flower of the flax. This is being grown again on the Brendons and elsewhere and is the base for linseed oil and linen.

ST MARY'S – This village is part of the Old Cleeve parish and the church was not completed until 1910.

CLEEVE ABBEY – There is a free car park and the Abbey is entered by a bridge over the Washford river and a walk up to the Gatehouse built in the thirteenth century. Over the doorway is a motto in latin – PORTA PATENS ESTO. NULLI CLAUDARIS HONESTO – which translated reads 'Gate be open, shut to no honest person'. The building was originally of two storeys; the upper floor would have been for administration. One can still see the almonry, where the poor money would have been handed out. Opposite is the Porter's Lodge. On going through the Gatehouse and looking back the visitor can see the statue of the Virgin with the Child. The Abbey was founded by William de Romare in 1198 and the first monks arrived here from Revesby in Lincolnshire, headed by their leader Ralph. They called the area 'Vallis Florida', or Valley of Flowers. The Cistercians took their name from Citeaux in Burgundy. The building of the red sandstone Abbey began in 1198 and was completed by 1297. These monks were farmers and they carried on their simple life of work and prayer,

Cleeve Abbey: the gatehouse.

weaving habits made from the wool of their own sheep which roamed the moor. The monks were highly thought of; they helped the poor, ministered to the sick, preached in the churches and welcomed visitors. The closure of the Abbey was a great loss to the

The River Washford flows outside the Abbey.

community. There were seventeen monks residing there in 1539. After the Dissolution part of the Abbey was turned into a farmhouse and kept in use, which is probably why it is one of the best preserved abbeys in England today.

CISTERCIANS – This order of monks wore white with no adornment at all. They believed that all things including prayer should be of the purest possible form. They became known as the white monks. They were opposed to all forms of greed. They built some beautiful abbeys across the length and breadth of Europe.

OLD CLEEVE – Old Cleeve means craggy cliffs. The area of Cleeve was given to the monks in 1202. The village lies between the Washford and Pill rivers.

Chapel Cleeve was founded in the fifteenth century when the chapel of St Mary was built to replace one destroyed in a landslip in 1452. On the south side of the chapel was an inn which served pilgrims attending the chapel until the Dissolution. Part of this inn was incorporated into a new dwelling which then became Chapel Cleeve Manor.

Bardon House, or Old Cleeve House as it is sometimes called, has a long history. There is a reference to the house as early as 1398. It was renovated by the Victorians in 1878 when they took off the thatched roof and replaced it with slate, and gave the house a new white-fronted look. Many minor skirmishes have been fought around it.

Its most famous story is that Robert Leigh, who lived at Bardon from 1595, hid a bundle of papers connected with Mary Queen of Scots in the attic. These became known as the 'Bardon Papers', the bundle consisting of six letters and legal papers marked 'Concerning the Q of Scottes'. Now in the British Museum they became famous for suggesting that Mary was not involved in various plots against Elizabeth.

The Leigh family remained in the house from 1595 until 1924. In about 1830 a servant saw a white dove fly into an attic window shattering it. Mr Leigh was angry and did not believe her story. The window was repaired but shortly afterwards was again found smashed and once again the dove had been seen. On a third occasion the dove was seen by Mrs Leigh smashing the window. A few days later, she died and Mr Leigh boarded up the attic. In 1834, after getting over his grief, Mr Leigh agreed with his son and daughter-in-law to re-open the attic. In a trunk beneath a lot of rubbish, the letters concerning Mary Queen of Scots were found. People believed that the white dove was Mary, trying to find the correspondence.

There are some lovely trees in the garden of Bardon House, including a very old Spanish chestnut, a lime and a magnolia; a pomegranate and other creepers climb over the white walls.

Also in Old Cleeve the John Wood Tannery is an interesting place to visit. There one can see sheepskins actually being converted from their natural state through the many skilled processes to the finished article.

ST ANDREW'S CHURCH — The porch floor of this fifteenth century church is set with pebbles collected from the beach at Blue Anchor.

In the north wall is the effigy of an unknown man with a cat and mouse at his feet carved from Beer stone.

This stone is quarried at Beer, in south east Devon. These quarries are fantastic. For a small fee one is taken inside, to find an area the size of about three cathedrals. The first people known to mine there were the Romans. There are stories of smuggling and contraband. The names and initials carved through the ages are people who worked there. During the 1800s, mushrooms and rhubarb were grown in the caves and sent up to Covent Garden.

In St Andrew's there is a beautiful coloured window in the south wall of the chancel. It was made by Charles Eamer Kempe. On each anniversary of his birth, June 19th, 1837, flowers are placed in the church. The name Kempe is famous for coloured glass and people come from all over the world to see this window. Kempe always left his signature – a wheat sheaf – in the corner of his work. There is a flourishing Kempe Society which keeps records of all Kempe windows.

The church tower was built by the same mason who worked on St Decuman's at Watchet.

An unusual feature about the church is the new gargoyle which is made in the likeness of the present rector, Rev. Hugh Allen. This can be seen as one leaves by the lych gate.

BLUE ANCHOR – Previously known as Cleeve Bay, in the late eighteenth century it became a bathing resort known as Blue Anchor. The first thing one notices is the long sandy beach and the multitude of caravans. This holiday site first opened in the 1930s.

The promenade is three-quarters of a mile long. It is said that a low water spring tide exposes the remains of a submerged forest. The kelp weed which grew in abundance was sent to the Bristol markets.

This is another station stop for the West Somerset Railway, on its way to Minehead.

There is a story that on the shingle shore of Blue Anchor Bay the splashing of oars or the swish of sails could sometimes be heard, followed by footsteps and whispering as smugglers made their way up the beach to two horses complete with black plumes and a cart containing a coffin. It was bad luck to look upon this procession as it was said death would then come within the year. Superstition was rife in the early nineteenth century and so the pirates carried out this ghostly adventure time after time. Anyone investigating too closely was paid off with brandy. The booty was hidden in local houses, farms and churches.

Smuggling reached its height during the Napoleonic wars, especially in the west of England, which was an easy trip from the continent. The loss of revenue was great and with war looming the authorities were so concerned that it was thought to be a national danger.

Along the beach towards Watchet some of the marbled alabaster mentioned before can be picked up at low tide.

Two good refreshment stops are the Blue Anchor Inn on the hill, which has been in existence since 1678 and the Smugglers on the promanade.

BILBROOK – This pretty little hamlet is spoilt by the traffic on the main road running through it. The little brook which babbles along is called the Pill. The eighteenth century Dragon House was once one of the main smuggling hideaways. Today it serves scrumptious food. Have a look at the minstrels' gallery in the domed inner room and the colonnaded sunken courtyard and extensive gardens.

* * *

Here I have my own story to relate. My daughter's friend, Teresa, came to Somerset for a week from Eastbourne. Teresa is psychic and several times she has had visions of the past and future. My daughter and my son decided to take her for a meal in this area and whilst eating Teresa suddenly became very quiet. Later my daughter became quite warm and went over and opened the window. Teresa immediately got up and shut it. My daughter thought she was acting a bit strange but tried to ignore it. Later when they were walking out to the car park, Teresa kept looking over her shoulder and she couldn't get into the car quickly enough. When they got home my daughter asked her if she had felt alright. 'Yes,' she said. 'It was just that there was a monk watching us eat, at least he looked like a monk, but he was wearing white and monks only wear brown or black. He had a horrible face as if he was violent or had received violent treatment. He followed us back to the car and watched us drive off.'

My daughter didn't tell her that the Cistercians wore white and had lived in the area.

* * *

CARHAMPTON — Legend has it that during the Dark Ages this area, which consisted of dense forest and marshy bogland edging down to the sea, was terrorised by a dragon which carried off children, adults and animals. It was hunted by many including King Arthur. One day a man made his way out of the sea and up the shore, dragging a bundle of stones. He then set them up in a triangle and preached to the local people. He told them his name was Carantoc, a Welsh prince who had denounced all earthly riches and set sail across the Severn Sea to be put down wherever God wished him to be. He was asked if he could rid them of their dragon, so Carantoc waded out into the sea and called the dragon. It came up to him quietly and he wrapped a sash around its neck and led it amongst the people. He then told the dragon to go away and not to annoy these people any more. In repayment a chapel was built and dedicated to Saint Carantoc.

There was a settlement here from early times and St Carantoc's church was a 'missionary' church. In AD 1180 the church was given to Wells Cathedral. The same church served the parish until well after the reign of Edward II. In AD 1300 a new church was built and dedicated to St John the Baptist.

Saint Carantoc was a bishop and a confessor, and was heir to the kingdom of Ceredigion, now Cardigan, in Wales. He became the patron saint of Carhampton, Llangranog in Wales, St Crantoc in Cornwall and Tregarantec in Brittany. His feast day is celebrated on 16 May.

Both King Egbert (died AD 839) and King Ethelwulf (died AD 858) were involved in campaigns against the Danes, who invaded Carhampton in AD 836 by sea and again in AD 843. On both occasions the Saxons lost heavily. Later another King of Wessex, King Alfred the Great (AD 871), owned the estate and he willed it to his eldest son.

Carhampton is another village that lies astride the busy A39 road. The public house is the Butcher's Arms. Marshwood Farm is Elizabethan and a former residence of the Luttrell family.

A large red sandstone house lies near the church. It was formerly the vicarage and in 1928 workmen dug up several skeletons. The way they were lying suggested that it was a former churchyard.

Carhampton was once important enough to give its name to the hundred or administration centre of 18 parishes.

Wassailing of the apple trees is a very old Somerset tradition and Carhampton is one of the places where this practice continues.

A walk to the west along a bridle path leads to Dunster, and another footpath to the south west leads to Withycombe Hill and on to Luxborough.

ST JOHN THE BAPTIST – Midsummer's Day is the feast day of St John the Baptist to whom the church is dedicated. It was rebuilt in red sandstone between 1862 and 1870 by the Victorians. The old Norman font was then replaced by a square font which displays arum lilies on each side. Despite Victorian interference it still retains a fine old fifteenth century Perpendicular appearance. There are remains of the original wagon roof in the south aisle and an extremely fine fifteenth-century screen. The screen stretches right across the church, still bearing all its bright colours.

The churchyard is reputed to be the largest in Somerset with a footpath running through it which was once used as a cart track. The very bottom of the old preaching cross also remains here.

DUNSTER – Dunster is actually in Exmoor but for the purpose of this book Dunster falls within my own boundaries and thus the Brendons.

The candlelit week-end, always held the first weekend in December, is well worth a visit; the houses display candles in the windows and all the electric lights in the shops are replaced by candles. It is festive and romantic, although in our day and age it can also be a catch-penny.

Just walking down its main street is an adventure with the little tea shops selling home made cakes and pastries, and the Olde Worlde gift shops selling lovely local work. The architecture is well worth some study.

In 1377 Dunster had a population of 163 when Wells was the largest town in Somerset with 900 inhabitants.

As one approaches from the sea the first building of note is the Luttrell Arms Hotel, a sixteenth-century coaching house. It was previously known as the Ship Inn but prior to that it was the Abbot's House for Cleeve Abbey. It played quite a significant role in the Civil War, as Colonel Blake's Roundheads stayed there during their 160-day siege of the Royalist-held castle. Cannon balls fired during this siege damaged the Yarn Market.

The octagonal market was erected by George Luttrell in 1609, following an Act of Parliament governing the sale of cloth. Dunster, like Taunton and Bridgwater, had its own cloth called Dunsters. Building of the Yarn Market meant that traders could stand under cover to carry out their business. It was extensively repaired in 1647 after the siege. There were Shambles by the Yarn Market but they have long since disappeared.

When Leland visited Dunster in 1541 he wrote that:

> Dunster Toun stondith in a Botom. The glory of this
> Toun rose by the Moions that were the Erles of
> Somersete.

John Leland was educated at St Paul's School and then Oxford and Cambridge. He became one of the Royal chaplains and King Henry VIII gave him a living near Calais and appointed him keeper of the library. In 1533 Henry authorised Leland to travel the kingdom with power to search 'England's antiquities, and peruse the libraries of all cathedrals, abbeys, priories etc, and places where records, writings, and secrets of antiquity were deposited'. In 1546 he presented the King with his collection and the design of the works that he intended to produce. King Henry VIII died in 1547 and on his death Leland fell distracted; by 1550 his mind was deranged and he died in 1552. The manuscripts became dispersed. The first edition of the *Itinerary* re-appeared in 1710 in nine volumes.

From the High Street there is a short climb to the castle. First built in the eleventh century, it originally had two irregular 'keeps' united by curtain walls and two semi-circular bastion towers, nothing like the present building. It is the town's outstanding feature. The de Mohuns were given the estate by William I after the Norman Conquest. Some landowners, the favourites of William the Conqueror, had many estates bestowed upon them. William de Mohun acquired 68 manors.

The de Mohuns held the Castle against King Stephen in favour of the Empress Matilda during the Civil War.

At that time the sea line was much nearer the town than it is today. The National Trust guide to Dunster Castle reads: 'A twelfth-century account of the Tor describes the impregnable defences of the place, inaccessible on the one side where it was washed by the tide.'

The main roadway into Dunster would have been by way of Gallox Bridge. The easiest form of transport from here was by boat and it is recorded that trading with Spain and Italy took place from Dunster harbour in 1338. Gradually over the years the River Avill silted up and the beach drifted further away.

The castle was sold to the Luttrell family in 1376 for £3400. The castle was rebuilt in 1617 when George Luttrell engaged William Arnold to design a new house in the lower ward of the castle. After the Civil War it was again refurbished when Colonel Francis Luttrell installed fine plasterwork ceilings and a new staircase. Between 1868 and 1872 Anthony Salvin was employed and made the biggest alterations, making the castle much as it is today. It remained with the Luttrell family until given to the National Trust in 1976.

King Charles II, when Prince of Wales, stayed there for a fortnight in 1645 to escape the

The Luttrell tomb in Dunster church.

plague which was rampant in Bristol and further east. Charles was fifteen years old at the time and he had been sent to Bristol after the defeat of Marston Moor to try to raise new levies and drum up support for his father.

There were two reasons why he stayed at Dunster for only two weeks; the plague had now spread to Dunster, and Dunster Castle was the only Royalist stronghold in Somerset, so it was too dangerous for him to remain.

Here a personal story is related. One of my friends is a guide at Dunster Castle. One day, four very well dressed Arabs came in, two ladies and their husbands. They pointed to the appropriate passage in the guide book and whispered to my friend:

'Is it possible to arrange for us to meet Prince Charles, we will make it worth your while?'

She replied 'I am sorry but he is dead!' This caused much consternation among the group.

The Conygar Tower was built on the opposite hillside in 1765 at a cost of £192. It was not only a popular folly of the time, but was also used as a landmark for shipping. There is a lovely walk to the tower from the A358 lay-by near Ellicombe.

There is a working water mill with twin overshot wheels at the rear of the castle. The mill has changed little in 900 years although it was considerably restored in 1680. Later it fell into disrepair and was not used for many years. In the Second World War it was used once more to grind flour for the nation's bread. After the war it nearly fell into ruin until Mr Capps leased it from the National Trust in 1978. There is a tea room, a museum and a mill shop.

Dunster's sixteenth century dovecote was in commercial use until 1870.

It produces stoneground wholewheat flour and is one of the finest working mills in the West Country. The mill is situated alongside the River Avill, where the Domesday Book recorded two water mills but more were added later, the others now long gone. Until 1790 this river was running two fulling mills, six grist mills and one oil mill.

Dunster's dovecote was used from the Middle Ages to breed pigeons for the tables of the wealthy. Dovecotes, also known as columbaria, pigeon houses or culveries, were used up to the eighteenth century to provide fresh meat in the form of squabs (newly hatched chicks) or pigeons. By the seventeenth century there were about 26,000 dovecotes in England. Inside Dunster's dovecote there are places for 500 or more nests which are reached by a wooden revolving ladder. The dovecote can hold 2000 doves and was used until 1870. Some historians believe that it was built in the late sixteenth century.

The Butter Cross was previously in the High Street. On market days it was used for the selling of butter as its name suggests. It was moved to its present site in 1825.

The village garden is a beautiful and peaceful place where one can sit and relax. In the early twelfth century William de Mohun gave the lands for a Benedictine priory which was served by a prior and 13 monks. It prospered until the Dissolution. In 1543 Lady Margaret Luttrell bought the land for £85.16s.8d. and on her death in 1580 it passed to her grandson George Luttrell. This area then became the kitchen garden to the castle. After it fell into disuse the villagers held a collection and bought the garden in 1980, turning it into the lovely peaceful area which is enjoyed to-day.

Another lovely Dunster garden is behind the church, a garden of remembrance. The plaque reads 'The Church Garden which is dedicated to the men of Dunster who died for their country'. In the garden is a well, with the dedication: 'Given to the church

Dunster: the Luttrell well in the lovely Garden of Remembrance.

Dunster's Old Nunnery was in fact built in the fourteenth century by local monks to accommodate visitors.

and people of Dunster by Geoffrey and Alys Luttrell for all time. Easter 1953.' It is not to be confused with the Holy Well near the Butter Cross and marked on the Ordnance Survey map.

There are some interesting buildings in Church Street. One is the Priest House, a timber-framed sixteenth century cottage supposed to have been built from ships' timbers; it is by the entrance to St George's Churchyard. It was restored in the nineteenth century.

The Old Nunnery is a fourteenth-century three-storey building, built by the monks of the Priory for their guests. The house was previously known as the Chantry of St Lawrence and acquired its present name in 1796 – no one knows why, as there were never any nuns in Dunster; with such a name it makes one wonder who their guests were!

Harwoods of Dunster have their establishment here and claim to be the original patentees of the first automatic wrist watch.

The Methodist Church is dated 1878 and has a Flemish-Baroque facade.

METHODISTS – Methodism began at Oxford University when four young men became friends and started meeting regularly to read from the Bible. One of these young men was John Wesley (1703-81). The name was given to the group originally in fun, because of the methodical way in which they ran their lives. They toured the country preaching by market crosses and in fields. John Wesley wanted to send some of them to America to spread the word of God in the New World, but first he wanted them ordained as priests. The Bishop of London refused to do this, so Wesley assumed the powers of a bishop and ordained his preachers himself. This gave the preachers the power to administer the Sacrament of Holy Communion. The Church of England would still not recognise Wesley and his preachers, so they reluctantly started their own separate church.

BENEDICTINES – This first monastic order was founded in western Europe by St Benedict of Monte Cassino, near Naples. The monks had to take vows of poverty, obedience and chastity. The first group were introduced into England by St Augustine of Canterbury in AD 597. They wore black habits and each priory was a small self-contained community.

ST GEORGE'S CHURCH – The main body of the church, cruciform in shape, is fifteenth century. The tower, built on the foundations of the old Norman tower, was completed in 1443 by John Marys, a mason from Stogursey. He charged 13s.4d. per foot to build it.

In the 1400s a dispute arose between the monks and the parishioners, which went on for 30 years. The case became so involved that it went to arbitration at Glastonbury, where it was ruled that the church should be divided into two, one half monastic and one half secular. This led to the erection of a large screen which marks the division finally agreed upon. Part of the old smaller screen was supposedly sent to Raddington Church, but there is no evidence at Raddington to support that supposition.

The magnificent oak rood screen, carved in AD 1500, is 60 feet long with 14 bays. Looking through the screen at the chancel and casting eyes up to the left, the visitor will see a French jester who fell ill there. Someone nursed him until he was better. He then went into the church and thanked God by juggling and doing acrobatics by the altar. He became so popular that he was remembered in that way.

There is a Norman west door and a thirteenth-century stone altar in the north chapel, the remains of an earlier building.

Plague victims were buried in the churchyard during the Civil War and when the slave

Gallox Bridge, Dunster.

trade was rife someone managed to acquire a negro, whom they christened in Dunster Church as William Dunster.

There is also a tithe barn in this area. Tithe means tenth and a tenth of everything the tenants grew had to be given to the Lord of the Manor, where it was stored in the barn.

At the bottom of West Street just before leaving Dunster, and turning left into Park Street one will find some more lovely thatched cottages, typical of villages in this county. Just beyond the car park is a packhorse bridge and a ford, spanning the River Avill. Gallox Bridge is medieval and was originally called Doddebridge. Gallox or Gallocks is a reminder that once there were gallows nearby; two Monmouth supporters were hanged there. Over the bridge and just past the one remaining building there is a cross pattern of footpaths leading to Carhampton, Luxborough and Withycombe.

There is also a circular walk of about three miles through beautiful deciduous woodland, a steady climb but well worth it. The road is known as The Old Coach Road, and built by Mr George Luttrell in the nineteenth century as a route to Luxborough and beyond. By the time it had reached the top of the hill it was proving too expensive and the idea was abandoned. At the top the road bears left, and there is, a little way on the left, a footpath turning back up the hill. Take this and after about 100 yards a gate and a stile on the right leads up through woodland and a short climb to Gallox Fort.

GALLOX HILL FORT – This Iron Age enclosure is perfectly preserved, with a deep ditch and with what would have been earthen walls above that. It would have had small huts, probably round, and several animals; in fact a small hilltop community. Back on the main track walk downwards and then upwards again to Bats Castle.

BATS CASTLE – This fort is believed to be Iron Age but was later inhabited by the Romans, then known as Caesar's Camp. Again one can clearly see the deep ditch, 130 feet in diameter, and completely round. It is thought that at some stage it was enlarged. It was probably last used as a fort during the Civil War, when the eastern entrance was made. It would have been a strategic stronghold, looking down on Dunster Castle and towards the coast. Any approaching ships would have been seen clearly. It was much easier for goods and people to travel by sea than it was by land.

On the main track again, one soon comes to cross roads and a pine forest. Take the left down the hill. There is a line of beech trees and a stone wall on the left, known as the King's Hedge. It is not known which king this refers to but it could relate to the boundary set during the Civil War. Near the bottom of the hill one can turn left again into a field which is part of the original deer park of Dunster Castle. The Luttrells created the deer park in 1755 to supply the castle with fresh venison. Several properties had to be bought, leases terminated and tenants moved so that the park pale could form the enclosure. Walking on again one soon comes to the stile and the crossroads at Gallox Bridge, where the walk started.

TIMBERSCOMBE – The meaning of its name is obvious 'a valley of timber'.
Bickham, which lies to the west, was once the medieval manor house. It is mentioned in the Domesday Book, as 'Bichecome'.

Saint Petrock was an abbot who became the patron saint of Timberscombe and many other parishes in Devon, Cornwall and Brittany. He was the Chief Saint of Cornwall and Apostle of Dumnonia.

Timberscombe Victoriana: a stone drinking trough for animals.

A stone animal drinking-trough dated 1876 stands by the steps leading to the church-yard. The inscription is now well worn: 'Everyone that Thirstent ... to the Waters'.

The village pub is the Lion Inn where one can be sure of a welcome.

The School House has a plaque which reads:

> To Richard Elsworthy - MDCCXIV.
> Who gave this school for the
> Education of the poor in the
> Principles of the
> Church of England.
> LAUS DEO.

The primary school is situated behind this house.

ST PETROCK — Welcome to St Petrock's Church, Timberscombe,
I hope that you are enjoying the beauty and
the quietness of this church where our Lord
Jesus Christ has been worshipped for over
1,000 years.

> The Vicar.

This is the welcome on the church door. It was said that the holy man, Petrock, also came across from Wales on a raft with his cow and settled in Timberscombe. The fifteenth-century church was a 'missionary' church in early times. The Perpendicular tower, dated 1708, has a pyramid roof. A wall fresco has been partially uncovered to show St David playing his harp.

CUTCOMBE — This village is mentioned in Domesday. It is 6 miles long and 3 miles wide, bounded on the south by the Hare Path and taking in the Dunkery ridge (1700 feet) and Lype Hill (1400 feet). The village itself is 1000 feet above sea level and the highest village in Somerset.

Hare stories seem to crop up in this part of the world and in the village I found one more. Fanny Pope once lived there with her grandson, in Heathpoult Cross Inn just up the road above the village. The boy was always able to provide hunters with a fine hare to chase, for which he would be given a shilling. He always ran with the hounds. One day the hounds were gaining rapidly on their quarry and the boy shouted 'Urn granny, urn or they'll catch ee.' This made the huntsmen very suspicious and when they returned to the Inn they found Granny Fanny bleeding and panting and near to dropping. Hares were always associated with witches and when witch hunting was at its height in the Middle Ages many such fanciful stories were believed.

Legal enclosure of Common Land took place during the eighteenth and nineteenth centuries and Cutcombe Common was enclosed in 1797.

Alice King, a blind author who wrote stories with an Exmoor background, lived at Cutcombe. She also started a bible class for 70 men and boys, founded the brass band and encouraged the cricket team. The fifteenth-century cross was renewed in 1898 as a memorial to her father, the Rev. John King.

Cutcombe itself is joined to Wheddon Cross and they are practically one and the same, sharing post office, shop and pub. On the confluence of the roads is Cutcombe Church of England Primary School.

The church is down the road beside the school marked 'No Through Road'.

Mr Webber, one of eight children, remembers the Lady of the Manor, Lady Winifred Bouverie, giving presents at Christmas to all the poor children. She also left three cottages to the church. His father, William Henry Webber, was one of three village tailors who used to work in a little shed in the village which they called the ferret box. One day Henry Hales P.Bouverie told him it was much too small for a village tailor and he built him the house called Dunkery View in 1908. Mr Bouverie also did a lot more building for his tenants at that time. Mr Webber's brother, Sydney, was the clever one so he took up tailoring after his father; the rest became farmers. Later Sydney became a farmer as well, and although he developed a crooked spine, he still managed to stand upright. The doctors in Exeter Hospital were so intrigued with this that they showed him as an example to young doctors. Sydney was a noted cricketer and footballer and he became the Parish Clerk. He died in January 1993.

In the 1880s a brass band was formed in Cutcombe, its members coming from Bridgetown, Winsford and even Withypool. They played as far away as Dulverton and Haddon Hill and they travelled in two horse carts.

The foundation stone of the present Methodist chapel was laid on 29 April, 1893. The previous chapel was just up the hill on the B3224 where Chapel Cottage stands today.

An interesting character was William Francis Melhuish who was born in Cutcombe in 1842 and died in 1913. In 1858, aged sixteen, he joined the Electric and International Company in Taunton. He rose to become its Director in India, and in 1894 was the first person to use wireless telegraphy for commercial purpose. This was when the underwater cable between India and Ceylon broke and contact was maintained by radio for nine months.

ST JOHN THE EVANGELIST – This thirteenth century church stands on a bank overlooking the road. The gargoyles (hunky punks) on the tower stare back, one has a drain pipe sticking out of his mouth. Inside the church one immediately gets the feeling of antiquity. At the end of the north aisle is a coloured glass window in memory of the Bouveries, mentioned above.

There is a plaque on the south wall to John Myres King AM (also mentioned above), Vicar of the Parish for fifty-five years. He was a scholar of Balliol College, Oxford.

A tombstone outside the churchyard door reads

John died Nov 2nd 1901
Aged 8 years and 2 months.
Also
Minnie died Dec 9th 1910
Aged 7 years and 9 months.
Also
Ivy died Dec 19th 1910
Aged 5 years and 10 months.
The beloved children of
Thomas and Alice Priscott
of Higher House, Cutcombe.

These children died of diphtheria. Infant mortality was very high until the Second World War: before this time diphtheria, whooping cough and tuberculosis were killer diseases.

WHEDDON CROSS – Adjoining Cutcombe village, the hill is also the watershed between the River Avill which flows north and the River Quarme which flows to the south and joins the Exe. The public house, situated on the top of the hill is called The Rest and Be Thankful. One can go horse-riding with Jon Trouton at North Wheddon Cross Farm where there is an Outdoor School with teaching facilities and many more attractions. There is hardly a better way to see the hills than in the saddle.

The villagers held a meeting and with the backing of the West Somerset District Council decided to create a colourful mural on the outside of the public toilets. It has been worked in mosaic.

Snowdrop Valley is along the Avill but still in this parish.

Cutcombe Fair was always held in mid September and there is still a special sale on that day in the Auction Field.

It was walking down the valley that I spotted the following notice and I wondered if anyone else had seen the spelling mistake:

> Putham Qarry,
> No Dumping,
> Max. Penalty,
> £2000. S.C.C.

BRIDGETOWN – This little hamlet, which is in the parish of Exton, lies by the River Exe. The public house is called the Badgers Holt Inn. The disused chapel is now residential, dated 1848. There are two old bridges just past the chapel.

The village has always been known for producing a good local cricket team.

Just north the River Quarme runs into the River Exe and south of the village is a bridge known as Chilly Bridge.

EXEBRIDGE – Just north of this lively little hamlet, the River Barle flows into the River Exe and it is from this river, which has its source way up on The Chains on Exmoor, that the hamlet takes its name. The river flows quietly by, lapping the beer garden of the Anchor Inn, another highly recommended hostelry. That was not always the case; the dark and dreary night of Friday August 15, 1952 remains in the memory. No one thought that the peaceful Exe could cause such havoc and destruction. For four weeks it had been very wet and on the previous day nine inches of rain fell in 24 hours. The Chains up on Exmoor soaked up that deluge of water like a giant sponge and when it couldn't absorb any more the Chains let the water go. Millions of tons of water poured off Exmoor, flooding all the valleys. Everyone has heard of the consequent Lynmouth flood. The Exe valley suffered too. At Dulverton a wall of water came down the valley, covered the bridge, and went straight through the garage by the bridge, taking several cars with it. When the water reached Exebridge it filled the valley, flooding the ground floors of the houses. Some eye-witnesses reported that a wall of water 7 feet high came down the valley; others said the wave was 14 feet high. Thirty-four people died, eleven of whom were holiday makers.

There is also a large trout farm, Exe Valley Fisheries; taking the lane on the right after crossing the bridge by the pub, one can see it in return for a donation in the collecting box.

The bridge itself is very old and its highest point is the boundary between Devon and Somerset. Because the hamlet is divided between the two counties, the Devon part belongs to the parish of Morebath and the Somerset part to the parish of Brushford.

There is a manor house near Brushford called Combe. In the 1680s, Major George Sydenham, who owned the house then, had several discussions with his best friend Captain Dyke. They liked to discuss the existence of life after death and whether or not there was a God. One night they agreed that whoever died first, would come back on the third day, either in ghost form or by doing something the other would recognise. On the third night they would sleep in a certain part of Combe. George died first and Captain Dyke slept in the agreed place, where he remained undisturbed. Several weeks later his ghostly friend appeared. 'I am sorry I could not come at the agreed time,' he said, 'but I am here now to tell you there is a God, a very just and terrible one and I advise you now to turn over a new leaf.'

The round house on the edge of Exebridge, dated 1830, was once a toll house. It is now let as a holiday cottage.

The road from Exebridge to Bampton winds over a steep hill, known as High Cross. It is supposed to be haunted and mightily uncanny in the dimpse time. (Dimpse is a Devon word for the half light or twilight).

BAMPTON — The Britons had a small settlement beside the River Batherm roughly where Briton Street is today. Later they enlarged it, calling it 'New Town' and it extended to Newton Square. In AD 614 the battle of Beamdune was fought at Bampton between the Britons and the West Saxons. It was a vicious and bloody battle and over 2000 Britons died. By AD 712 a church was built. It belonged to Glastonbury Abbey.

There is a recreation field on the north-east of the village called 'The Moat', on the site of the old castle moat. In the field a mound with a rookery was once Bampton Castle. The castle no longer exists but probably several castles were built on the same site, possibly as early as 300 BC.

At the Conquest the land went to Walter of Douai. In Domesday it had land for 25 ploughs and a mill and was valued at £18. Domesday also records that Bampton had 353

Luke Street, Bampton: the peace and quiet of the nineteenth century.

pigs – a very valuable asset and well worth counting. They foraged in the woodlands and common ground on acorns and beech nuts and were then slaughtered at the beginning of winter. They were salted down or smoked and would then feed the inhabitants throughout the cold season.

A motte and bailey structure existed by the reign of King Stephen. The castle was besieged by King Stephen when the rebel Robert de Bampton owned it; the country was locked in Civil War over whether King Stephen or the Empress Matilda should reign.

During that period the Hunting Law was well established with severe penalties for poaching in a Royal Forest. Simon, the Miller of Bampton, a poacher, is described as 'an habitual evil-doer to the venison of the Lord King'. I couldn't find out if he was one of the men caught and executed, but many men did meet such a fate.

In 1336 Richard Cogan owned the castle and was allowed to crenelate it, normally permitted after a man had been to battle or gained some great honour. From the Cogans the manor passed to the Bourchiers, Earls of Bath, who were the last owners to live at the castle. Their emblems and coat of arms included a reef knot, which has been used in various ways in the village, including a motif on the blazers of the Bampton School children, and a 'water bouget', which consists of two water sacks which could be slung over a donkey or similar beast.

During medieval times the village held a weekly market and two fairs. The Pony Fair, which obtained its charter in 1258 during the reign of Henry III, is held on the last Thursday in October. Ponies were rounded up on Exmoor on the Saturday before the Fair and were later herded all the way to Bampton; in the present century they were brought in lorries. The selling of ponies has now been banned completely.

A railway known as the Exe Valley Line ran through here from 1848 onwards, from Dulverton to Exeter. It was part of the G.W.R., or 'God's Wonderful Railway', and the little steam engine was known locally as the 'Tivvy Bumper'. The last train ran in 1963.

Bampton Fair, 1916.

At the turn of the century No.47 Brook Street was an inn, known as The Great House. After closing, it became a guest house and then a private residence.

Elizabeth Penton started a school for poor children in 1821 in National Terrace, Brook Street. This later became a National School. An infants' school was built by subscription in 1836 in Western Way, off the churchyard, taking infants up to six years old. In 1938 a new Secondary School and a Primary School were opened in West Street and the National School was sold. The churchyard school, on loan to the Secondary School, opened again for a short time during the war, and later it was used as the woodwork room. It was eventually sold in 1965.

In 1909 the following was read out by the village crier on the steps of the Post Office:

The introduction of state pensions was welcomed in style.

PROCLAMATION
By R.S.Webber, Bampton, Devon.
On Old Age Pension Day, January 1st 1909.
REJOICE!   REJOICE!   REJOICE!

A Happy New Year to all and every person who is entitled by law to receive the pension placed at their disposal by a noble act of this RADICAL GOVERNMENT for the better treatment of the aged deserving people who have spent their lives for the good of the state.

His Majesty the King has willingly assented to the measures, and everyone can receive in Cash now at the Post Office.

The genial Post Master will be delighted to meet and pay over the cash to those entitled at 8 o'clock. GOD SAVE THE KING and may this GOVERNMENT long continue in office to carry out THOSE OTHER REFORMS that this country requires for the benefit of the working classes.

GOVERNMENT OF THE PEOPLE
FOR THE PEOPLE   BY THE PEOPLE.

The village has won the 'Britain in Bloom' competition on more than one occasion and is now known as the Town of Flowers.

The River Batherm runs through the village and joins the River Exe just before it reaches Cove. The source of the River Batherm is just north of Bittescombe Manor near Sperry Barton. The name Batherm in Saxon means 'A bathing place for the poor'.

On 24 August, 1858 a licence to obtain rocks from the stone quarries called Little Kersdown and Bampton Old Wood Quarry was applied for. Bampton stone contains chert and flint, excellent stone for roads. At the time the Kersdown Rock, comprising half an acre of land, was owned by Thomas Cross. The quarries were then bought by Sir Edwin Dunning during the late nineteenth century and Archibald Scott became the manager in 1905, later buying the firm. Scotts (Bampton) Ltd were once one of the main employers in the village. During the 1914-18 war and earlier, quarrying limestone was mainly from Bampton and Whipcott. Later, hardstone was taken from Wonham, Highleigh and Cove.

The house now called Hillcrest used to be the stables for mules and ponies which pulled the stone on drams all the way from the woodlands which lie across the road from Kersdown Quarry to Ashleigh House; from there the trucks ran downhill to the crushing plant. The stone was lifted up to the woodland from Kersdown by a small engine and pulley. During the 1920s the drams went out of use and steam lorries (Fodens and Sentinels) did the job. Burnt lime was produced at Bampton for many years, collected by farmers with horses and carts. In 1920 the roads in the village were tar sprayed for the first time by Scotts.

Frank William Bowyer, an engineer, came to Bampton in 1926 to install a large 150 H.P. Blackstone Oil Engine for the crushing of stone. That engine also gave the first electric light to Bampton by means of a shed which held batteries situated above the engine. The batteries were charged for the Exe Valley Electricity Company.

On the Orkney Isles a memorial marks the 75th anniversary of the first aircraft to land on the deck of a moving warship at sea. The pilot was Squadron Commander Edwin Dunning, who was the son of Sir Edwin Dunning of Stoodleigh Court, the former owner of Bampton and Whipcott quarries. Unfortunately Commander Dunning was killed when trying to make a third attempt five days later.

In 1924-25 excavations were made at Bampton Reservoir, off High Street, and new cast iron water mains constructed and laid through the streets. All the excavations were done by hand using picks, shovels and wheelbarrows.

When the Second World War began, all able-bodied men signed on and a Home Guard was formed by the older generation. Land Army girls came and worked on local farms. Evacuees were billeted in all available spaces, organised by the Rev. Jones, the Baptist chapel minister.

Stone from the quarries was used to build airports at Dunkeswell, Exeter and Chivenor.

Bombs were dropped in a field between Bampton and Morebath, when a damaged German bomber unloaded his cargo, and an enemy bomber came down in flames at Tucking Mill, the site of ancient tucking mills on the Bampton to Tiverton Road.

In 1975 road widening on the B3190, Bampton to Frogwell Lodge road, made better access for construction vehicles involved in the making of the new Wimbleball Dam.

ST MICHAEL AND ALL ANGELS – Here again there is evidence of habitation throughout the ages. The tower is thirteenth century, the chancel fourteenth, the nave fifteenth, the pulpit and beautiful wagon roof sixteenth, and so on, each century leaving its mark. On the pulpit is the face of a man with his hair set on end. He is 'Jack in the Green', an ancient fertility symbol. He can also be found over the small window in Culbone Church on Exmoor. The Bourchier knot can be seen in the screen and the roof bosses. From the thirteenth century onwards the wool trade brought wealth, and many churches were enlarged. This church was no exception and the north aisle was added. The pillars and arches of the aisle are made of Beer stone.

One of its best remembered vicars was the Rev. Bartholomew Davey, M.A. He went to Blundells School, Tiverton, and then on to Balliol College, Oxford and King's College, Cambridge. He married an heiress, Jane Govett of Tiverton and he was appointed vicar of Bampton in 1785, where he served for fifty years until his death.

When the church was restored workmen found a vault where the organ now stands; it contained several coffins believed to be those of the Bourchier family. On the north wall of the chancel are the remains of one of those coffins, that of Tomasine Bourchier who died on 3 July, 1453; the two Bourchier emblems mentioned above can be found in its carving. (See Norton Fitzwarren).

One thousand years old and still going strong: yew tree in churchyard of St Michael and All Angels, Bampton.

There is yet another ditty in a book on show there, this time from a previous vicar:

> The parson is a wored out,
> The Clerk is most ado,
> The Sextons gude for nort,
> Tis time to have all new.

The Victorians in their restoration took the roof off and a careful look shows that the large beam is narrower at the tower end where it was difficult to fix back on.

The two big walled-up yew trees which stand outside the church are reputed to have been planted during the reign of Richard III. Yew was then much used for archery. Those trees live longer than any other species in Europe; many are thought to be over 1000 years old. Early Christian missionaries preached under them long before their first churches were built, indicating that many churches were built on a

A plaque to the clerk's son, killed by a falling icicle.

spot already devoted to worship. It is thought that these trees were walled up to stop sheep grazing in the churchyard from eating the poisonous yew. I was also told that they were walled up during the last century to stop them falling over.

A plaque in the bottom of the tower marks the spot where the Parish Clerk's son was killed. He was standing close to the wall, head back looking up the tower, when an icicle fell off and pierced his eye, killing him. It reads as follows:

The Clerk's son -

Bless my iiiiii
Here he lies
In a sad pickle
Killed by icicle

SHILLINGFORD – The school was once a Board School. The public house is called the Barley Corn and the Baptist chapel is dated 1888. There was a chapel of ease near Dipford Farm, but all that remains today are the foundations. The stones were taken and made into a wall in the garden of the Old Vicarage, Bampton; at the same time two fonts were also removed and are now by the stocks in Bampton churchyard.

PETTON CROSS – Here, scattered houses and farms are set in beautiful countryside with a picture-book church called St Petrock's. The church was rebuilt in 1848 on the site of an older Norman church. Two thirteenth-century bells, taken from the old church and

Medieval fonts from Dipford Farm, now in the churchyard at Bampton.
installed in the new building, still call people to worship after seven hundred years.

WATERROW – The Rock Inn, a four-hundred year old tavern, resting house and good eating house is literally built into the rock. Before 1851 it was known as the Rock House Inn. The Brendons behind rise some 400 feet to Chipstable.

Waterrow: the village on the hillside.

The road that runs over Yeo Bridge from Wiveliscombe to Bampton was once a turnpike road.

The Devon and Somerset Railway opened here in 1873 and a large iron viaduct was built, becoming an outstanding landmark in the area. Trains from Wiveliscombe travelled across the viaduct and then passed through a tunnel to Venn Cross Station. Venn Cross, like Waterrow, is still in the parish of Chipstable. The railway line closed in 1966 and the tunnel was then used to grow mushrooms. The iron viaduct was demolished during the 1970s, only the pillars remain.

Manor Mill, an eighteenth century water-mill, sits beside the River Tone. It has now been converted into holiday accommodation. Hurstone Farm Hotel is also a restaurant and Halsdown Farm is a working farm with much to offer.

WIVELISCOMBE – This thriving little market town lies on the south side of the Brendon Hills. While doing research I read one of the loveliest conjectures I have heard as to how the town acquired its name. 'In Saxon times, the combe was always abundant with weevils ['weevil' being the Saxon word for insects], and so this town became known as Weevilscombe.'

Long before the Norman Conquest, the Manor belonged to a man called Wilfa or Wifela, and many think the name comes from that: 'Wilfa's combe.'

King's Castle is a prehistoric camp, one mile east of the town covering 12 acres. On the opposite side of the valley is a smaller camp called Minnington Park Camp. Roman coins were found on Castle Hill in 1711. After the Roman presence the Danes and the Saxons both took over the castle in their day and Saxon remains have also been found.

The Palace Gate, Wiveliscombe.

The Manor was granted by Edward the Confessor to the See of Wells. In the Domesday Book, Wiveliscombe is recorded as held by the Bishop of Wells, with land for 36 ploughs.

In AD 1256, Bishop Button obtained a charter of 'free warren' for himself and his successors from Henry III. John de Drokensford then built, or rebuilt, a stately palace behind and adjoining the cemetery, south of the church. In 1331 Ralph of Shrewsbury improved the palace. Today all that remains is the fourteenth-century archway of the gatehouse, which once led to a green appropriately named the Palace Green. The inside arch of the gatehouse was removed and is now around the main entrance to the library. In 1735 a workhouse was erected on part of the site of the ruined palace and since then private houses have gradually taken all the space. The windows of the palace were put into the school house.

Queen Elizabeth took the Manor away from Bishop Godwin of Wells and gave it to Sir Walter Ralegh. This was a punishment for the Bishop for marrying a twenty year-old girl when he was already an old man. 'Thomas Godwin was made to part with the Palace, "out of necessity and not by choice", he parted with the Manor for a term of 99 years to purchase peace and quiet.'

Bournes House was built by Bishop Bourne, 1554-60, and later passed to his brother.

In medieval times, the town was granted authority to hold two markets a week and three fairs a year.

The housing estate is known as Plain Pond after the large ponds which supplied fresh fish to the Bishop's Palace.

During the Civil War when the country was ravaged by plague (mentioned under Dunster when the Prince tried to escape that pestilence), Wiveliscombe suffered very badly, with its inhabitants confined to their houses to try to stop the infection. The people were impoverished and starving. In 1646 the Somerset Assizes ordered that all parishes and tythings within a five mile radius of the town should pay rates of £20 per week to get the stricken town back on its feet. Between October 1645 and August 1646, 468 people died in the town.

In 1688 Elizabeth Colles died and left money for almshouses for eight poor and aged people. Elizabeth was the daughter of Humphrey Wyndham who lived at Golden Hill and the wife of John Colles, The Barton, Corfe. She is buried with John in Pitminster Church, but one of her sons is buried with Humphrey in Wiveliscombe.

At the time of the Monmouth Rebellion several men of Wiveliscombe fought in the battle and later three were hanged in the Town Square.

The Town Hall and Market House was erected by Lord Ashburton in 1840. Corn was once sold in the Market House, a brick building with a spacious hall, portico and a balcony. At the rear there was room for the pig market.

The Congregational chapel was founded in 1662 and built in Golden Hill in 1708 and enlarged in 1825. The Methodist chapel at Lambrooke was built in 1845, while an iron mission chapel seating 100 people was in use at Langley in 1894.

In 1791, according to John Collinson, there was a well turfed race track two miles long on a hill called Main Down (Maundown), one mile west of the town. On the east of that hill is a spring which ran into a reservoir in West Street; from there the water was piped to most of the houses.

The name Langley Marsh means the long marsh meadow.

There were extensive slate quarries at Wiveliscombe, which have not been used since 1883.

In 1804 an infirmary was founded in High Street by William Hancock and Henry Sully with voluntary attendance by medical gentlemen of the neighbourhood. It was of great benefit to the poor.

In the eighteenth century Wiveliscombe was famous for its hats, made of rabbit's fur.

A railway line from Taunton to Wiveliscombe was opened in 1871, extended two years later on to Barnstaple. By 1874 it reached Ilfracombe. This line became known for the 'Rabbit Train' as there were so many rabbits in the area, and these were put on the train at each station and sent up daily to the markets in London. Like the others this line is now gone.

For quite a long time Fox Brothers of Wellington had a small factory in Wiveliscombe which kept several local men employed. Flemish immigrants also worked in the wool and lace trade.

*This Tudor-style home of local brewer and benefactor, William Hancock
was built in 1881 and now houses the library.*

The Tudor-looking building in the Square, now housing the library and other businesses, was built in 1881 as the home of William Hancock.

A free library and reading room was erected in 1887 in Silver Street, at a cost of £350, to commemorate Queen Victoria's Jubilee.

The *Wellington Weekly News* and *Wiveliscombe and Milverton Herald* were established in 1860 and printed on Wednesdays.

Abbotsfield, described as a fine mansion house, was erected in 1871 for Charles Lukey Collard, a well-known musician.

William Hancock's Brewery at Golden Hill was established in 1807, and became the largest brewery in the West of England. When William died in 1845 the business had expanded, with some 18 public houses in Wiveliscombe and the surrounding areas. His son William took over the business which continued to expand. In 1927 the firm amalgamated with S.W.Arnold & Sons with breweries in Taunton. Later the brewery was known as Arnold and Hancock. The new company bought a brewery in Crewkerne in 1938. By the outbreak of the war Willoughby Hancock had taken over. He let Abbotsfield, now the family home, as a convalescent home for wounded servicemen and went to live in a house next door to the brewery. The brewery horse, Prince, pulled the cart around the area delivering beer, but on Mondays his role changed and the cart served as the rubbish cart. The firm of Arnold and Hancock was sold to Ushers in 1955 and a few years later brewing ceased in Wiveliscombe. A bill sent out by the firm in 1939 shows two bottles of port priced at nine shillings (45p), and twelve flagons of ale fourteen shillings.

On June 12th, 1980 Golden Hill Brewery (on the same site as the old brewery) produced the first brew of Exmoor Ale. A cask of Exmoor Ale was entered in the CAMRA Great British Beer Festival at Alexandra Palace in London that year and the firm came away with the ultimate prize – The Best Bitter of the Year. They are now Somerset's largest brewery and Exmoor Ale, Somerset's real ale, is now sold throughout the southern counties.

The Cotleigh Brewery set up in 1979 at Cotleigh Farmhouse at Washfield, Tiverton moved to part of the old Hancock's brewhouse in Ford Road in 1980. Its output is now three million pints a year. At the Maltings Beer Festival, in Newton Abbot in 1993, Cotleigh Brewery won the championship in the standard bitter class – only one Championship of many that has been won by both these breweries. Cotleigh name their three regular beers after birds of prey, the original and most famous is Tawny.

Wiveliscombe County Primary School built in 1876 is an attractive building with a lovely tiled roof. Kingsmead Comprehensive School was developed from the Secondary Modern School built in 1953. It became Kingsmead Community School in 1987.

The large car park in the middle of the town is free.

St Andrew's Church – In 1292 the church was valued at 40 marks. Holy Trinity, the old medieval church, was pulled down in 1827 and rebuilt in red sandstone by the Somerset architect, Richard Carver, at a cost of £6000. In 1829 it was dedicated to St Andrew. The cost was borne by the parish rates and spread over twenty years.

At that time the Norman font was placed outside and filled with flowers as a garden ornament. Later it was recovered, mounted and given a lavish oak cover, and used as a font once more. The register dates from 1536.

There are monuments to the Wyndhams, dated 1622 and 1620. In 1915 a rose window was put in.

There are catacombs under the church and during the Second World the church played a very important role, storing many ecclesiastical treasures, including gold, silver, glass, plate, books, pictures and furniture. Much of these valuables could otherwise have been destroyed in the bombing of cities.

Ford – This hamlet is in the parish of Wiveliscombe. There were once three mills there. There are some nice residences including Ford House.

The Quaking House – All that can be seen today is a Friends' Burial Ground from 1681 which apparently was used a few years ago when the ashes of a Quaker were buried there. In 1679 Francis Brayne and Nathaniel Attwood purchased a plot of ground, which was part of a field called Havershill, from Edward Pole. In 1681, Francis Brayne, an apothecary in Wivelis-

The Norman font at
St Andrew's Church, Wiveliscombe.

combe, passed the plot of land to the Trustees of the Society of Friends. A chapel was never built there; before the Toleration Act (1689), prayer meetings by different sects were forbidden. There were two cottages nearby where the Quakers started having private prayer meetings. In 1692 Sarah Cheevers and Alice Hellier were sent to gaol for holding such a meeting in the Quakers' Meeting House, now referred to as the Quaking House.

When Edward Pole died in 1762 he left ten shillings yearly to be used to repair the Meeting House in the Burial Ground. The Wiveliscombe tithe map of 1841 shows a building in the burial ground called Quaking House. The present Quaking House is a house called 'Warrens' and it is some little way away from the burial ground. It used to be two cottages, then it was a farmhouse, so presumably that is the original building. There is no evidence of there ever having been a building in the burial ground.

In 1753 it was decided to build a meeting house in the town of Milverton and Thomas Pole bought a plot of land for that purpose. The house in North Street was built by 1760.

MILVERTON – A charming village mentioned in the Domesday book, it then had a mill at the side of the Hillfarrance Brook which paid 7/6d. per annum.

One of the oldest houses is 'The Old House' also known as 'The Parsonage'. It was built in 1480 as the counting house for the Archdeacon of Taunton. It underwent major reconstruction in the 1500s. The most famous Archdeacon of Taunton was Archbishop Thomas Cranmer, but there is no evidence that either he or Wolsey ever lived there. After he became Archbishop and moved to London, Thomas Cranmer annulled the marriage of Henry VIII to Catherine of Aragon in 1533. As Archbishop he was head of the Roman Catholic Church in England but when the monasteries were dissolved, he changed his allegiance and became the first Archbishop of the new Church of England. He encouraged the translation of the Bible into English and in the reign of Edward VI he compiled two Anglican prayer books.

When Bloody Mary, the daughter of the Spanish Catherine of Aragon, a Catholic, came to the throne, Cranmer was condemned as a traitor and heretic. In 1556 he was burnt at the stake in Oxford. In Taunton a street and a school are named in his honour.

Alterations were made to 'The Old House' in the eighteenth and nineteenth centuries. The house became a vicarage for seventy years until it was commandeered during the Second World War. It is now a private residence, Grade II listed.

In 1685, 62 men marched from the town to join the Yellow Regiment in support of the Duke of Monmouth, who had all his regiments named after colours.

North Street boasts some lovely Georgian houses. At the north west end and to the rear of Ivy Cottage, is a large house built in 1760. It is approached by a cobbled courtyard. This was the Friends' Meeting House where Thomas Young was a prominent founder member. It was regularly used by the Quakers until 1855. It was sold by the Society of Friends to Ann Young (a relative of Thomas Young) in 1872. Occasional meetings were held there until her death in 1902 when the Quaker connection ceased.

Doctor Thomas Young, born on 13 June, 1773 in the house now called 'The Old Bank House', was a famous scientist known for his Wave Theory of Light. His study of Egyptology led to the deciphering of the Rosetta Stone.

Thomas Fox ran a Quakers' school in the High Street. Quaker children from all over the country came to be educated, at a cost of £35 per annum.

There was a devastating fire in Milverton in 1708 which destroyed several houses in the Sand Street and Faircross areas.

ST MICHAEL'S CHURCH – On the north side of the churchyard the Broadmead family planted some cedar trees to mark the burial site of the plague victims of 1645 to 1667. These were felled after the heavy storms of 1978-79, but new ones have since been replanted.

This church is built in red sandstone and dates from the fourteenth century except for the base of the tower which dates from AD 1200. The pulpit was built in 1928, but sixteenth-century panels were inserted into it.

PRESTON BOWYER – This Manor was once held by the Count of Mortain.

A farmer named John Joyce who lived there was the man who persuaded the West Somerset Farmers' Club to allow an NFU branch to be formed in Taunton in 1918.

A cottage known as 'The Chantry' stands on or near the site of the old Chantry Chapel. After the break from Rome the practices of saying prayers for the dead and holding masses were forbidden by Henry VIII by Act of Parliament in December 1545. In 1547 King Edward replaced it by another Act to dissolve all chantries, and all endowments were confiscated, much of the proceeds going to Edward Seymour, who was the Duke of Somerset and The Lord Protector at the time. Some of his friends also benefited. In all, 2374 chantries were suppressed.

HILLCOMMON – A hamlet again spanning the main road with two good eating houses, The Baron of Beef and The Royal Oak. The Royal Oak, about one hundred years old, used to be a cider house. As late as the 1950s horses and carts would be tied up outside while the farm labourers had their cider.

NORTON FITZWARREN – On the hill behind the church is a circular 13-acre iron age defensive encampment with 15-foot ditches. It was in continuous use until Roman times and large enough to hold a sizeable population and its livestock. It is thought that at that time it was called Theodunum. When the Saxons fought the Britons the encampment was used again. A dragon was believed to live in the area, spreading terror and death throughout the parish; it is depicted on the screen in the church with a female in its mouth.

It is said of Norton that:

> When Taunton was a fuzzy down,
> Norton was a walled town.

After the Norman Conquest the manor passed into the hands of the Fitzwarrens. The Lord Fitzwarren title, after several generations, passed to Fulke Fitzwarren and he died without issue. The estate then passed to his sister Elizabeth, who was married to Richard Hankford. They produced only one daughter, Thomasine who married William Bourchier, Earl of Bath so adding to his vast estate. She was buried in Bampton Church as mentioned earlier.

The Manor House of Norton Court now belongs to the Ministry of Defence and is used as the Officers' mess. (See Norton Manor Camp).

The Congregational chapel was built in 1821.

The Village Club was erected in 1896 by W.G.Marshall at the cost of just over £1000. Built of brick with Ham stone dressings, it comprised a large hall for meetings, a reading room and a smoking room. In 1897 a large bowling alley was added.

Arthur Moore, a cider maker, was approached by Pallett Bros in 1911 to help make cider

The Manor House, Norton, now belongs to the Ministry of Defence
and is used as an officers' mess.

at Norton Fitzwarren on the present site of the cider company. Taunton Cider PLC grew from this partnership. Now the second largest cider maker in England and famous world wide, they make 18 different varieties of cider.

The apples are pressed in large presses and when all the juice is extracted the residue, which is called pomace, is used for cattle feed.

Wassailing the apple trees is a pagan tradition supposed to ensure a good crop. Taunton Cider resurrected the custom about 20 years ago. The ceremony is held in January before old twelfth night. A Wassail Queen is chosen every year. Carried shoulder high into the orchard, she puts toast, soaked in mulled cider, into the branches of the trees. All the company that go with her beat two sticks together to ward off evil spirits and men also fire guns into the trees.

Cider has been made in Somerset since the thirteenth century and at one time it was part of a farm worker's wages.

The Wassailing Song goes as follows:

> Old Apple Tree,
> Old Apple Tree,
> We wassail thee, and hoping thou wilt bear,
> For the Lord doth know where we shall be,
> Till apples come another year,
> For to bear well and to bloom well,
> So merry let us be,

Let every man take off his hat and shout to thee,
Old Apple Tree,
Old Apple Tree,
We wassail thee and hoping thou wilt bear,
Hat-fulls,
Cap-fulls,
Three bushel bag-fulls,
And a little heap under the stairs.

Another folklore tradition survives when the apples are picked and a few are left on the trees, for the fairies and pixies, known as the 'Pixie Hoard'. It also ensures a good crop in the coming year.

After a management buy-out, Taunton Cider was successfully floated on the London Stock Exchange in the 1990s. Now 95% of the employees own shares in the company. The company employs two Master Cider Makers, a position achieved after a ten-year apprenticeship. It takes time to acquire the delicate tastes and smells. The two Cider Makers are not allowed to travel anywhere together in case of accident.

By 1919 the village was growing and one of the biggest employers was the Norton Mills Company, high class bakers and self raising flour manufacturers.

During excavations for the railway a great deal of Roman pottery was found. In 1890 a train accident in the village killed ten passengers and a further accident in 1940 killed 27. In the later accident the train was full of soldiers going home on leave. The crash was heard all around, some said as far away as North Curry. The landlady at the Ring of Bells in the village took the casualties into the skittle alley where she tore up her sheets to make bandages. One soldier had a rail across and through his legs and had to have both his legs amputated on the spot to free him. He became quite a Taunton character. He used to busk in the centre of town after the war, working a barrel organ; having no legs he had brass plates fitted just below his knees.

Many American soldiers were stationed at Norton Manor Camp during the Second World War. The fields beyond Station Road were very boggy, and it was said that years before a horse had actually disappeared into the bog. The Americans bragged about their Jeeps and said they could cross any terrain. Young local lads bet them that they couldn't cross the boggy fields beyond Station Road. Of course they tried; at first the Jeep kept going, then slowly it sank into the bog, right up above its axles. As the boys went home for the night, bidding a hasty retreat, big heavy cranes were being brought in to lift the Jeep out.

Burnshill was the name of the railhead for Norton Manor Camp during the war (814 Ordnance Base Depot). These Americans were there during 1943 and 1944 and used the Cross Keys public house as a local. At Christmas they gave a party for local children, supplying chocolates, sweets and toys, all of which were on ration and hard to get in England. They also held dances which many local girls attended.

Norton Fitzwarren is another village astride the busy road; it was once the A361 and the main road to Barnstaple until a new link road was built in the 1980s, running from the M5 Motorway at Tiverton. The Norton Fitzwarren road then became the B3227, but the traffic through there is still steady. The former army camp on the south side of the road is now a trading estate.

ALL SAINTS CHURCH – Another extremely beautiful building. Made of grey sandstone, it is of the Decorated and Perpendicular style. The first vicar recorded was in 1219 and the embattled tower dates from Richard II.

The church is entered by the lych gate, which dates back to 1913 and was put there in memory of one of the Wyndham Slades of Monty's Court. A local tradition is still maintained today: when there is a wedding, local children tie up the lych gate; the bride then has to be lifted over, but only after coins have been thrown to the children.

'Lych' is an old word meaning where the body rests.

The churchyard was a favourite burial ground of the Somerset gypsies who were mainly interred in the south-west corner.

The rood screen is spectacular, one of the best carved in Somerset. It stretches right across the chancel. The whole screen kept its colouring until 1825 when it was covered with a coat of oak varnish. It has now become semi-transparent again and little patches of colour can be seen. The name Raphe Harris, a church warden until

The grey sandstone church of All Saints, Norton Fitzwarren.

he died in 1509, is inscribed on the screen, which may have been his work. He is buried in the west end of the church. The screen was once thrown out as rubbish but luckily it was rescued in 1886 by the rector of the time and restored to its present glory.

The clock was given in memory of William Henry and Frances Mary Hewett in 1925, but a presentation order prohibited a clock face on the exterior of the tower. However, permission was given in 1953 to commemorate the coronation of Elizabeth II. About ten years ago the villagers complained because the clock had stopped but were told there was no money available to repair it. Eventually Taunton Cider Company said they would donate three quarters of the cost to celebrate their jubilee year if the villagers raised the other quarter. This of course they were pleased to do.

I was reminded of another children's story here:

The teacher asked the class, 'Who is God'?
One little boy quickly replied 'Harold.'
'Why Harold?' asked the teacher.
'Our Father which art in Heaven,
Harold be thy name,' replied the boy.

At this point our outline tour ends as we reach the corner of our triangle and the Cross Keys Inn. We now have to fill the triangle in.

Chapter Two

The Right Hand Corner

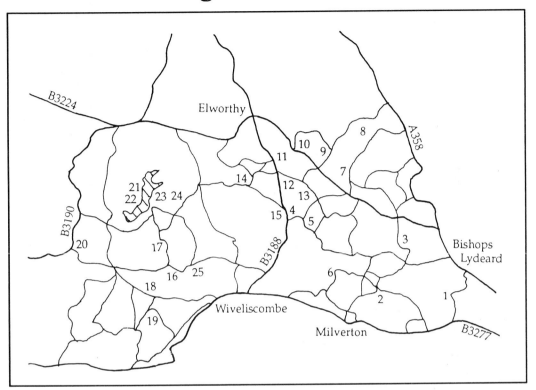

1. Tone Vale
2. Halse
3. Ash Priors
4. Scarr
5. Tarr
6. Fitzhead
7. Lydeard-St-Lawrence
8. Crowcombe Heathfield Station
9. Tower Farm
10. Willett
11. Willett Tower
12. Tolland
13. Gaulden Manor
14. Brompton Ralph
15. Pitsford HIll
16. Washbattle
17. Huish Champflower
18. Haydon Hill
19. Chipstable
20. Lowtrow Cross Inn
21. Clatworthy Reservoir
22. Syndercombe
23. Milltown
24. Trout Hatchery
25. Maundown

TONE VALE – One of the Luttrells built a house, Venn House, in these attractive grounds alongside Halse Water, and the foundations still remain. Venn House was mentioned by 1618 and in 1759 peaches and nectarines were planted. It is also said that there were cellars under the fishpond. More buildings were constructed in 1893 and in 1897 The County of Somerset and City of Bath Lunatic Asylum for paupers, Copford, was established. It could take over 700 patients. In 1948, it was taken over by The National Health Service as a psychiatric hospital. Tone Vale Hospital was closed in 1995 and a number of houses are to be constructed in the grounds.

HALSE –This is a charming little village lying about 6 miles west of Taunton. In ancient times it belonged to the hundred of Taunton when Halse was known as Halse Priors. At the time of Edward the Confessor the estate belonged to Ailmar, a thane of distinction. William the Conqueror took the Manor away and gave it to one of his favourites, Roger Arundel.

Roger still held it at the time of Domesday, in which it is interesting to note that the mill is mentioned; at that time it paid ten shillings per annum to the Lord of the Manor. Roger Arundel founded a nunnery. It was colonised by the sisters of the Convent of Tolland, eventually dissolved by Henry VIII. In 1227 a descendant of Roger Arundel, also called Roger, gave the manor to the Hospital of St John of Jerusalem on condition that they and their successors should found, support and maintain a chapel at Halse for ever. In 1290 the master of the hospital obtained from the Crown a charter to hold a weekly market on Mondays. In 1335 the manor, along with the rectory, belonged to the Knights Hospitallers and subsequently to the Priory of Mynchin Buckland which the Knights also founded. At this time the annual income of the manor was £10. The manor remained in their hands until the Dissolution of the Monasteries. Henry VIII then granted the estate to Alexander Popham and William Halsey. The family of the latter continued there for several generations.

By 1822 Halse was a parish within the Manor of Williton and Freemanners (by 1840 this was spelt Free Manors).

There was a village school by 1603 run by various charities. Edward Prior erected and endowed a school for boys and girls in 1848.

A small chapel was erected in 1840 for the Bible Christians; they later became the United Methodists.

Halse House, already standing in 1677, had descended to Samuel Gooding by 1716. It was completely restored during the next century and by 1830 was called Halse Manor. During the Second World War it was used as a boarding school. It was then sold to the Ministry of Health in 1952 and new buildings were added. By 1981 it was an overflow for Tone Vale and occupied by elderly psychiatric patients. It is now residential.

Nearby Stoford Farm dates from the thirteenth to fourteenth centuries. The main door and some plasterwork are Elizabethan.

There are many ancient walls throughout the village made of the local red sandstone.

ST JAMES' CHURCH – The Knights of St John built the church on the site of an old Saxon building in the thirteenth century. Here can be seen the marks of a scratch sundial, which is on the right hand side of the porch as one faces it. There is a small circle of tiny holes. In the days before clocks and watches the times of services were governed by the sundial; when the shadow of the gnomen (or in the case of the Mass dial a stick would be placed in the hole in the middle), reached a certain place the sexton would ring the bell and the service would begin. In England, with the weather poor and often no sun, many an argument broke out over services starting too early or too late.

Field Marshal Montgomery's uncle was once the Rector of Halse.

In 1900 the church was in a bad state and large scale restoration took place, instigated by the Rev. Montgomery. The ends of the pews were carved by the village lads. In the east window a number of small sixteenth-century Flemish medallions were left to the church by a private collector.

ASH PRIORS — At the time of Domesday this village was called Aisse, meaning Ash. The land was held by Giso, Bishop of Wells in 1066. Giso was the last Saxon Bishop of Wells.

The Domesday Book records that the manor was held by Roger Arundel. He was the son of Roger de Montgomery, Lord of Montgomery, a town which lies to the south of Lisieux in France.

This parish is the smallest in the district, with only 640 acres. The village lies to the south west of Bishops Lydeard and became known as Priors Ash because the Prior of Taunton had a house and a court there surrounded by ash trees, which stretched to Ash Common, a small grassy area to the south of the village.

The Priory Manor House remains with a two-storey porch. The date, 1529, is carved in one of the spandrels of the four-centred head of the doorway. It is believed that King Alfred once owned this site and he made a gift of it to one of his knights.

The Priory is a listed building. It is said to have a 'Priest Hole'. The listing refers in particular to the front face including the porch and to the pillars at the front gate. There is said to have been a tunnel between the Priory and the church used by the monks at the time of the Reformation.

Francis Arundel Winter lived in the Priory in 1838 when the tithes were defined.

Village calm at Ash Priors: the smallest parish in the district.

A date stamp set in the converted farm buildings of the Priory marked 'J.W. 1841', is believed to refer to John Winter who also lived in the Priory. It was John Winter who gave Taunton the Cricket Ground, and also built the 'Winter Folly'. (See Combe Florey).

Later Mr Charles Antony Onley Saville-Onley, lived in the Priory. He was an engineer and had one of the earliest dynamos installed in the garden. His wife lived in the Priory until she died in 1950, at the age of 90. Mr and Mrs Antony St John Webster then bought the Priory.

The monks had other cottages and buildings but they were all screened from the Manor House by trees. There are still rows of trees there today.

At the end of the road the footpath called 'The Monks' Walk', crossing Ash Common, was named by Mr Valentine St John Webster after a clairvoyant who had been staying in the village said she saw monks walking along the track.

It is known that the monks did actually walk that way from the quarry with their horses and carts loaded with stone. They returned with the carts full of manure.

The barns near Monks' Walk were used by the cattle drovers as an assembly point and resting place on the way to Taunton cattle market from Exmoor.

Ash Common, a green area of 50 acres adjoining the village, has been made into Taunton Deane's first local Nature Reserve on a ten year management scheme, with the agreement of the owner Mr Williams, and with help from the Grand Met. Trust and English Nature.

The Old Mill is an attractive building and set into the walls along the front are old mill wheels. The water is the Denbury Leet Mill stream.

On the Dissolution of the Monasteries in 1539, Thomas Arundel administered the Court of Absolution, and the board gave all the inhabitants of the Priory House and cottages 2/6d per year to move elsewhere.

Later the Lords of the Manor were the Lethbridges of Sandhill Park.

In 1549 one Roger Sempson lived in the village. He was a very well known west country bell founder, and always stamped his initials on his bells.

By 1866 there was a small school for boys and girls supported by voluntary contributions.

Another interesting fact is that the population in 1801 according to the Census was 155, while in 1981 it was 95.

The ancient walls around this village can easily be identified as they are of crumbling red sandstone dating from the sixteenth century.

The last hill of Exmoor is said to be in Ash Priors, and there is a direct line route from Ash Priors to Ralegh's Cross. There is a public footpath through Ash Wood from Denbury all the way to the Friendship Inn above Lydeard St Lawrence.

An old public house in Ash Priors, known as the Park Gate Inn, is now a private residence.

HOLY TRINITY CHURCH – This is a small church dating from the twelfth century. It was restored in 1874.

SCARR AND TARR – Tarr is a hamlet with very few buildings. It belongs to the parish of Lydeard St Lawrence. Nearby 'Scarr Chapel' lies in a valley with a brook running through it. There was once a working quarry belonging to Kings, who built the Independent Chapel for the workers. When the quarry ceased to be used a manse was built adjoining the chapel. Behind the manse is the disused quarry.

At the bend in the road a footpath marker reads 'Gaulden Manor ¹/₄ mile'.

FITZHEAD – This village adjoining Wiveliscombe to the north east was mentioned in the Domesday Book as part of the Wiveliscombe manor. Early Lords of the Manor were Canon and then Southby. Lord Ashburton was the Lord of the Manor by Victorian times and his manager lived in Fitzhead Court, a Georgian house with a good seventeenth century plaster ceiling displaying shells, palm leaves and cherubs. It also contains the coat of arms of the Canon family, who were resident until after the time of Charles II.

The wool industry was a major employer and in 1682 an Act of Parliament was passed as follows that: 'In the 4th year of the reign of our Sovereign Lord Charles the Second all people must be buried in sheeps wool only'.

A Church of England School was erected for children of both sexes in 1850. The village cricket club was founded by the Rev J.N.Watts in 1902.

In 1908 the old buttressed tithe barn in the churchyard was bought by the village for £100 and converted into a Church Room and Village Hall.

Lime was extracted from the nearby hills and burnt here for agricultural purposes and on one of the roads out of the village a lime kiln can still be seen.

In the churchyard is the Rockwell Stone dedicated to William Rockwell by his American descendants. He was baptized in Fitzhead in 1590.

ST JAMES' CHURCH – The church was rebuilt, with the exception of the tower, by the Victorians in 1849. The building is of red sandstone with a Perpendicular west tower. There are many monuments to the Canons and the Southbys who lived there until the seventeenth century.

In 1745 the sum of five shillings was paid for ringing, rejoicing in the Duke of Cumberland's victory over Bonnie Prince Charlie.

In 1761 the following notice was recorded by John Collinson.

> May ye 20th at a public vestry this day it was consented & agreed
> that ye N & S side of ye church should be plaistered & ruff
> casted and likewise ye S side of ye tower to be plaistered
> as much as is needful and whitewashed all over.

The four small, colourful church windows along the north aisle read:

> No.1. I was sick and ye visited me.
> No.2. I was naked and ye clothed me.
> No.3. I was thirsty and ye gave me drink.
> No.4. I was hungred and ye gave me meat.

LYDEARD ST LAWRENCE – Lydeard St Lawrence is a large village supporting lots of small hamlets such as Rich's Holford, Treble's Holford, Coursley, Nethercott, Pyleigh, Chipleigh, Deane Hockham, Westleigh and Tarr. These hamlets mainly consist of a farm and perhaps one or two cottages.

The village was mentioned in Domesday and was given at the Conquest to William de Mohun. It went to various owners during its time. Combe Florey held it once but the most interesting Lord of the Manor was Edward Seymour, High Sheriff of Somerset and Lord Protector of the young King Edward.

According to Collinson, Lawrence was the second Archbishop of Canterbury and the village is named after him.

A spring rises behind the church and the water was once thought to have medicinal properties and was taken for 'Scrophulous disorders'. A stream rising in Tolland also runs through this village.

A charter was obtained for a fair which was held in the village on 10 August.

In 1666 a large number of Roman coins were found in a buried jar, evidence which suggests that Romans inhabited the area.

By 1861 there was a school for both sexes probably held in someone's house. A School Board was formed on 26 November, 1875 by Mr William Robert Pearse of Court Farm, who became Clerk to the Board and Attendance Officer. The school was erected in 1877.

Court Farm house was burnt to the ground over 100 years ago. The present farmhouse used to be two cottages. The Agricultural Society was formed in 1860 to recognise long and faithful service to the industry and to give prizes for such activities as ploughing. By 1906 the village had its own 'bobby', Constable George Ashford.

Mrs Routley – one of the village's oldest inhabitants – told me a story about a friend of hers called Mr Norman who used to ride his horse regularly up to Brendon Hill and back. One day as he returned his horse dropped dead. 'Well he arnt done that afor,' he said.

A former Congregational chapel is now a private residence.

Pains Farmhouse used to be an old longhouse. This is now converted into three cottages called Paynes Cottages. There is a most unusual feature in one of them, a smoking curing chamber.

THE CHURCH OF ST LAWRENCE THE MARTYR – There is a sundial over the south door dated 1653, and one also known as a 'scratch dial' or a 'mass dial' to the left of the chancel door. In the chancel a very interesting piscina bears the heads of King Edward lll and his wife Queen Philippa. 1327-1377.

The church is Perpendicular in style and built in red sandstone. On the capitals of one of the pillars there are the keys and sword, referring to St Peter and St Paul, which was the Conventual Church of Taunton Priory, and to whom the living belonged. In the churchyard there is the tomb of a Mr Venn, Squire of Pyleigh who was a Master at Balliol College, Oxford. He presided over the trial of King Charles I and was one of the men who signed the warrant for the King's execution. The residents of Lydeard St Lawrence disapproved of his actions and turned the font in the church upside down and said that no more babies would be christened in the same font as Mr Venn. The font remains upside down

The upside-down font at Lydeard St Lawrence Church.

West Somerset Railway: Crowcombe Heathfield Station.

Section of Brunel's broad gauge rail alongside a normal width track.

to this day and babies are christened in its upturned bottom. With the restoration of the monarchy in 1661 men who signed the death warrant were charged with regicide. John Venn had died in 1658.

CROWCOMBE HEATHFIELD STATION – The station lies on the left hand side of the A358 road. The station boasts a set of broad gauge rails, Brunel's early work. The section of track from Crowcombe to Watchet was begun in 1859 but owing to bad weather and other hold-ups it was not opened until 31 March, 1862.

Several special events are arranged during the year by the railway company including the 'Santa Train', when young children can meet Santa Claus on the journey.

A youth hostel for the Brendons is also situated in this lovely wooded area.

TOWER FARMS – As one drives along the B3224 past the Lydeard St Lawrence turning there are two turnings on the right. The first is marked Crowcombe and Rexton, and the Cheese Farm. Tower Farms (Taunton) Ltd was founded in 1973 as a partnership with the White Brothers of Willett Estate and Mr Peters; they make an extra mature Cheddar cheese called Exmoor Extra, a Farmhouse cheese, a mild cheese called Quantock Maid and a traditional Cheddar. In 1991 they opened a cash-and-carry shop on the site. They also sell clotted cream, butter, yoghurts, eggs, potatoes and pork products. Half the milk for these products comes from their own four farms, the remainder coming from 14 other local farms. Goat's and ewe's milk is also brought in from nearby farms. The meat is all from their own farms although they do not kill or cure it themselves. They have every reason to be proud as on 6 July, 1992 they achieved registration under the prestigious international standard BS5750/ISO 9002, making them the first farmhouse cheesemakers to be recognised for quality of management and service, as well as excellence of products. They employ a workstaff of ten in the cheese making department.

WILLETT – The second turning on the right off the B3224 is signposted Willett and Higher and Lower Vexford. Willett is a small hamlet of about four houses and a farm in the dip of the hills. Someone there has a sense of humour. A sign reads 'Please drive slowly, Free Range Children'.

There is a manor house, Willett House, with a long drive and two lodges, North Lodge and South Lodge, both now owned privately. The main house was built in 1816 and the parkland around it was created by 1840. This is a private residence, much loved and looked after by its present owner. It originally belonged to the Escott family of Stogumber and has been owned by the Cadbury's chocolate family. Beautiful old turkey oaks growing in the grounds are among its lovely features.

WILLETT TOWER – At 950 feet one can stand by this folly and look around 360 degrees at the Quantocks, the Blackdowns and Exmoor, whilst surrounded by the closeness of the Brendons. The red sandstone tower was erected in 1782 by Mr Bernard, Lord of the Manor of Crowcombe who died in 1811. The tower cost £130 of which Mr Bernard paid £80 and the rest was paid by subscription.

It was a steeple or marker for riders and it represents a ruined Somerset church or gatehouse. The tower can be approached from the B3224 Forestry Commission entrance to Willett Hill. Parking is limited.

TOLLAND – A stream which rises at North Combe, Brompton Ralph and runs through this village once turned a grist mill. It then flows on through Lydeard St Lawrence. It is said that the village actually gets its name from that stream which was called 'Tone' too, (*English Oxford Dictionary of Place Names*; E.Ekwall 1951). Old English 'Tan-Land'.

The village lies a mile from the turnpike road which led from Taunton to Dunster. The manor was held for the Bishop of Winchester by the families of Gaunt and Luttrell.

The Wolcotts lived at Tolland Mill, now called Watersmeet Farm. Henry Wolcott, his wife Elizabeth and three of their sons emigrated to Dorchester, Massachusetts in May 1630. The Wolcotts are commemorated by table tombs in the churchyard and a memorial in the two-light window in the west wall of the tower.

ST JOHN THE BAPTIST CHURCH – The thirteenth-century church, once called St Leonard's, welcomes one with the words 'Enter into his gates with thanksgiving'. I was also pleased to find that the greater part of the grass in the churchyard is cut only once a year; it is left to allow the wild flowers grow to maturity and to increase the butterfly population.

The church was given to the Priory of Buckland and after the Dissolution came into the hands of the Deanery of Dunster. Set around and under the altar are some medieval tiles.

The highly coloured later tiles in the sanctuary are from the church restoration in 1871. Here there are two more Kempe windows.

GAULDEN MANOR – A house of charm which is well worth a visit, it was originally believed to have been built around AD 1199. The present walls are thought to be medieval. It was three gifts of land given to Taunton Priory by Andrew de Boveden. About the time of the Dissolution of the Monasteries in 1539, Gaulden Manor became privately owned and has remained so ever since. From 1525 it was the home of Robert Sellack. John Turberville bought Gaulden Manor for his son, also called John, in 1615. John married Bridget Willoughby in 1639 and their two coats of arms are on the ornate overmantles in the hall and in the upstairs Hall Chamber. The magnificent plasterwork ceilings dating from 1640 are also accredited to these Turbervilles.

They are the family on which Thomas Hardy based his famous novel *Tess of the d'Urbervilles*.

During the Civil War the house lodged a detachment of Parliamentary soldiers. John Turberville wrote to his father in April 1647: 'The mansion hath been full of soldiers this fortnight, such uncivil drinkers and thirsty souls that a barrel of good beer trembles at the sight of them, and the whole house nothing but a rendezvous of tobacco and spitting.'

John Turbeville lived there until his death in 1677 when the house and estate passed to his eldest son, John.

The ghost of a lady appears from time to time on the staircase and there is also a lady in grey who sits by the fire, but it is not known whether they are the same person. A coach and four is said to be sometimes heard outside the front door.

It is believed that at one time a tunnel went from the house towards Wiveliscombe.

The house is open to the public. The present owners are ornithologists and interest lies with the garden, especially the pond with its ornamental waterfowl. There is a herb garden and a bog garden, plants are for sale and teas are served in the garden tea room.

BROMPTON RALPH – This well kept village lies at the east end of Brendon Hill and faces across the valley to Willett Tower. There is an ancient encampment which is accredited to the Romans.

In AD 729 Queen Frithogyth (wife of King Aethelheard of the West Saxons) gave the Manor of Brompton Ralph to the church of Glastonbury. This was held until William the Conqueror seized the lands and gave them to Sir William de Mohun of Dunster Castle.

During Domesday the manor was called 'Brunetune'. William de Mohun gave the Manor to his son Ralph, so adding to its name.

By 1861 there was a school for boys and girls. A Board school was built in 1877 for 94 children, covering Brompton Ralph and Tolland.

By 1861 there was also an independent chapel and two years later a new Gothic parsonage was built

There is a footpath from the village to Poolmill.

ST MARY'S CHURCH – The Parish is in the diocese of Bath and Wells and the church register dates from 1557.

The greater part of the church was built in 1738 and enlarged in 1847.

The lovely fourteenth century oak screen was restored to the memory of a parishioner, Robert Toms, by his grandson, an American.

Washbattle Bridge over the River Tone.

PITSFORD HILL – This is a hamlet belonging to the parish of Brompton Ralph.

WASHBATTLE BRIDGE – Located between Wiveliscombe and Huish Champflower, there used to be a corn mill here with a large water wheel. The mill ceased to grind in 1910. The River Tone runs under the ancient bridge and a track alongside the river takes one to Bulland Ford.

At the ford one can either walk through and up the lane to Heydon Hill or carry on across the road following the footpath into a field, then over a bridge and through the woodland on the right to Marshes Farm. Still keeping on the small track, continue all the way to Chipstable.

HUISH CHAMPFLOWER – Ailric held the Manor at the time of Edward the Confessor. It was then given to Roger Arundel but soon came into the hands of the Champfloryes (sometimes written Campo Florido) from whom the village gets its name. There was a de Campo Florido of Stert here in 1166, as well as record of Matilda de Chamflur in 1262 and a John de Chaumflour in 1349. The last owner bearing the name lived at the time of Richard III. His only child was a daughter who married Rafe Walensis, part of the family of Fantletoys of Dorset; much land was thereby added to the estate.

By 1840 the Lord of the Manor was Sir John Trevelyan of Nettlecombe Court.

The records state that in 1822 everything had to be carried on horseback as the roads were still not admitting of carriages.

The Castle Inn was built as a farmhouse in 1821 but it had become a public house by 1840. Today it is once more a private residence.

In 1857 a school was erected for boys and girls supported by the landowner and the rector. It was enlarged in 1895 to hold 100 children and became a National School.

In March, 1884 part of Chipstable, namely Chitcombe Farm and Withy, was amalgamated with the Parish for civil purposes, according to *Kelly's Directory of Somerset*.

The River Tone runs along the bottom of the village.

By the turn of the century the postman used to walk from Wiveliscombe each day to leave letters at the Post Office. A village postman would then deliver to each house and farm.

Two farms, Eastcombe and Westcombe, are believed to be haunted. Eastcombe Farm, established by 1515, has several different apparitions; the local quarries nearby were the scene of several deaths. Quarrying was carried out until the late eighteenth century producing good slates.

ST PETER'S CHURCH — A dissolved monastery, Barlinch Priory (sometimes spelt Barlynch), provided the materials and the windows for the aisle of this church. Most of it was restored in 1875 at a cost of £1100.

HEYDON HILL — One cannot help but admire the magnificent avenue of beech trees along this hill. At the end of the road, before rounding the bend to Chipstable, there is a small road with a sign which reads 'Bulland Ford. Unfit for Motor Vehicles'. Down there is Bulland Lodge where Air Vice-Marshal Capel once lived. His memorial is in Chipstable Church. Further down the lane in the valley is the ford (mentioned earlier under Washbattle).

CHIPSTABLE — The village is perched on the side of Heydon Hill. It was here at Domesday, as commemorated by a plaque at the entrance to the village. A cottage is marked 'The Old Police Station', but sadly there is no longer a local bobby. This cottage has a King George letter box in the garden wall.

There was a wheelwright called Poole, who set up the firm W.H.Poole & Sons. One son, Alfred, became a mechanical engineer and inventor, another son, William, also liked trying his hand at invention. They tinkered about with things like cars, telephones and photography. Alfred died in 1957; he was the last surviving son.

A pump house pumps water up to the village. There is a bore hole the size of a dinner plate which penetrates to the bottom of the valley and the water table. The water is then pumped up by electricity. It is tested regularly for its purity.

ALL SAINTS' CHURCH — In the centre of the village sits this beautiful church with some of the finest stained glass windows in the area. Ownership of the church was confirmed to the monks of Muchelney by 1239 when it was united with Raddington. The church is now joined with Huish Champflower and Clatworthy.

LOWTROW CROSS INN — A sixteenth century building, this inn is set in four and a half acres of unspoilt countryside on the edge of Exmoor. It is known for its own locally brewed ales.

The crossroads here was once the site of gallows.

CLATWORTHY — Clatworthy Castle is an Iron Age camp. It still has deep trenches which originally would have had palisades on them. Unusually it is triangular in shape. The bank rises some 15 feet from the base of the ditch, which would have been used both for defence and to keep out wild animals. The fort can be seen when walking around the perimeter of Clatworthy Reservoir. The woodland north of the dam formed part of the Clatworthy Estate and belonged to the Carew family.

A woman called Alviet held the manor at the time of Edward the Confessor. She paid geld for one and a half hides and there was land for seven ploughs. This was taken away by William the Conqueror and given to William de Mohun of Dunster Castle. The living was in the hands of Glastonbury Abbey. The manor of Clatworthy was mentioned in Domesday as the holding of William de Mohun but later came into the hands of the Arundels, as in 1227 Thomas de Arundel had a suit with the Abbot of Ford concerning land there.

In 1641 Parliament required every adult male, under oath of loyalty to King Charles I, to sign a Protestation 'to maintain and defend the true Protestant Religion expressed in the Doctrine of the Church of England, against all Popery and Popish Innovations'. The constables in each parish were responsible for collecting the signatures. The names of anyone refusing to sign were sent to the Sheriff. John Byam, parson of Clatworthy, was one who refused. He had his property seized, suffered a heavy fine and lost his living at Clatworthy. He also had a living at Dulverton which he managed to maintain by saying he had already passed the incumbency to someone else.

In this parish (described in 1791 by Collinson), was a hill called Beverton, where rises the River Tone. This turned a grist mill and then ran on under the stone bridge at Washbattle.

In 1948 a National School was erected for boys and girls.

Clatworthy Reservoir was built in 1958-59, filled during the following year and opened

Clatworthy Reservoir.

in 1961 by Princess Alexandra. The reservoirs on the Blackdown Hills were built around the turn of the century to supply water to Taunton. They were augmented by the River Otter. After the war, with the population of Taunton and district growing, these reservoirs became hopelessly inadequate and it was decided to build a new large reservoir at Clatworthy in the Brendon Hills. The headwaters of the River Tone were impounded to form this lake, which covers 130 acres and holds 1180 million gallons of water. In places it reaches a depth of 96 feet. The water runs by gravitational pull through a 24-inch water main down to Maundown Filter Station; it then supplies water to Taunton and the surrounding areas. The reservoir is a pleasant place to visit. There is boating on the lake for fishing. One can walk the nature trail all around the water or sit quietly on the picnic site and watch the world go by. No dogs are allowed. Canada geese are numerous and breed regularly.

SYNDERCOMBE — Syndercombe Wood is about one mile to the west of the dam and on the circular footpath. It was a hamlet belonging to the parish of Clatworthy. It derives its name from the accumulation of cinders from the furnaces of the Romans when they were smelting the iron ore.

Syndercombe House was described in 1432 as a mansion house. It was held by various families including the Hensleighs, the Periams and the Lethbridges. In 1874 it was described as being built of cob and thatched but by 1911 had been rebuilt in stone with a slate roof. When Clatworthy Dam was built in 1959 it was submerged along with other buildings in the area.

MILLTOWN — This is a little hamlet belonging to the parish, about a quarter of a mile to the west. It acquired its name from a working corn mill.

TROUT HATCHERY — Below the dam are ponds for brown and rainbow trout, bred for Wessex Water to restock their reservoirs by Mr Pursey and his son. A fisherman pays a daily rate and anything less than 12 inches long, or weighing less than one and a quarter pounds, is thrown back. The fish are bred in covered ponds to start with; then put into the open ponds, about 2000 fish per pond. It takes one million gallons of water a day to treat the ponds. Once the water comes out of the ponds it flows back into the River Tone below the dam. When the fish are two years old they are moved by a trailer tank to any of the authority's reservoirs. The tank holds a ton of water and is oxygenated. The fish can stay in the tank for up to six hours.

ST MARY MAGDALEN CHURCH, CLATWORTHY — This whitewashed Norman church was restored in 1865. It has a plain tower. The wagon roof is well worth seeing. The oldest bell is dated 1699 and inscribed 'Drawe neare to God'. The church register dates from 1558.

The whole of the porch, nave and chancel are paved with tiles made by the Agricultural Pottery Company, Poole. Rood loft stairs remain but there is no screen. In the churchyard are the remains of a medieval cross.

The church is in the diocese of Bath and Wells and the living comes under Chipstable.

MAUNDOWN — The Wessex Water Filter Station is located at Maundown. The water comes from two reservoirs, Wimbleball Lake and Clatworthy. About seven and a half million gallons a day comes from Wimbleball and seven millions from Clatworthy. Mr Peter Andrews said the water men watch the dams carefully and try to keep the levels as required. The water comes down from Clatworthy mostly by gravitation, although a booster pump is sited at the dam to aid the flow if necessary. At Wimbleball the water is pumped, as it is over in the next valley. Pumping costs between £6000 and £10,000 a month to run. The cost is off-set a little because the turbine at Maundown generates enough electricity to keep the plant going, which saves between £2000 and £3000 a month. The pipe which carries the water from the reservoirs to the filter station is buried about 3 to 6 feet deep.

The water is slightly acidic when it comes from the hills. Lime is added after filtration to neutralise this acidity and reduce the corrosive properties of the water.

Sodium silicate is also added together with chlorination. Alum is finally added to coagulate any particles left in the water, making them larger, so that the next filter plant can take them out. The final filter consists of sand plus anthracite.

The filter beds need periodical cleaning. Water is pushed up through the filter bed bubbling and oxygenating and is then drawn off. The sludge which is finally washed out of the sand drains into a skip. It is really thick and mud-like; it is then removed and used for land fill. The plant puts out 500,000 to 600,000 gallons of pure drinking water every hour.

Chapter Three
The Left Hand Corner

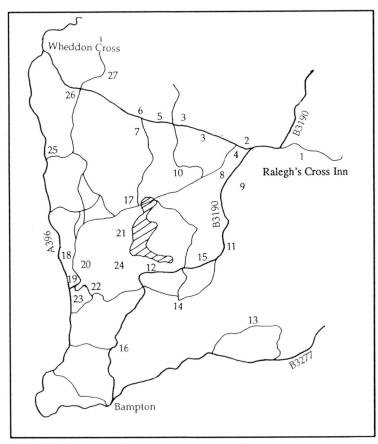

1. Ralegh's Cross
2. Brendon
3. Barrows
4. Beulah Chapel
5. Chargot Wood
6. Kennisham
7. Gupworthy
8. Beverton Pond
9. Middleton Court
10. Withiel Florey
11. Bittescombe House
12. Haddon Hill
13. Raddington
14. Skilgate
15. Upton
16. Morebath
17. Brompton Regis
18. Barlynch Priory
19. Barlynch Animal Sanctuary
20. Louisa Gate
21. Wimbleball Lake
22. Bury
23. Bury Castle
24. Hartford
25. Exton
26. Heathpoult Cross
27. Lype Hill

RALEGH's CROSS — The crossroad was once a five-road junction surrounded by very deep bogs. The stone cross guided travellers on the right tracks. It takes its name from the famous west country family; in 1387 after his campaign in France, Simon de Ralegh's body was left by the cross for the night on its way home to the manor of. Nettlecombe for burial. The plinth of the old stone cross by which the body rested can still be seen in front of the public house at Ralegh's Cross.

This sixteenth-century inn was once the stopping place for drovers and travellers with packhorses and goods on the main route from Bampton. Flocks of sheep were driven up and down the hills, and the August Auction Sheep Fair is still held in a field adjacent to Ralegh's Cross. Many thousands of local sheep are sold in that sale.

In the garden of the public house is a beacon. Read the story of the beacons and how they were lit and managed in the Middle Ages. The original braziers were part of a regular network of communications established to give news of the approach of an enemy at least from the time of threats of Spanish invasion in the sixteenth century to the Napoleonic Wars of

Ralegh's Cross: reproduction beacon from 1988 to mark the 400th anniversary of the transmitted news of the defeat of the Spanish Armada.

the late eighteenth and early nineteenth centuries. This reproduction fire beacon brazier was provided by the Somerset County Council in 1988 to mark the 400th anniversary of the defeat of the Spanish Armada.

Also in the garden is a pill-box from the Second World War, now discreetly hidden behind fir trees. Pill-boxes, like small martello towers, were built, camouflaged and equipped as strong points, their guns commanding the coast, or making a second line of defence between the south west peninsula and the rest of England, as it was thought that invasion might take place in the western counties.

Old photographs of the industrious days of the Mineral Railway line are displayed in the restaurant and bar. Parliamentary authorisation was given in 1855 to build a railway to Watchet harbour. It was completed to Ralegh's Cross in 1859.

BRENDON VILLAGE —Sitting on the fork in the road just past Ralegh's Cross is the Beulah Methodist Chapel. This was once a thriving little community and the miners in this area worshipped there. There was also another small chapel along the Wheddon Cross road called 'The Iron Chapel', but this is now gone. At the height of the industry there were 250 inhabitants of Brendon. Beulah Terrace, the main row of houses, is also gone.

At Burrow Farm the engine house can still be seen and the cutting along which the track ran is visible.

Take the Wheddon Cross fork (not the Bampton fork) and soon one can see the remains of a bridge which used to cross the road carrying the Mineral Railway. Walking here is difficult but the paths can be seen on the OS. map. The ruins of the wheel house, the cable house and derelict shafts are still at the top of the incline. The village stores is also now a private residence.

BEULAH – The chapel mentioned above was the miners' chapel standing 1,250 feet above sea level. An inscription on the outside south wall reads 'Beulah 1861'. It was opened by a Bible Christian Mission but is now Methodist and one of the few surviving reminders of the mining industry. When the mines were no longer viable and the railway closed, the chapel also closed for twenty-five years. It re-opened later.

BARROWS – Continuing along the Wheddon Cross road, Wiveliscombe Barrow, Cutcombe Barrow and Leather Barrow can soon be seen in the fields on both sides of the road. These are believed to be of the Bronze Age. They are clearly marked on the Ordnance Survey Map. Leather Barrow is the largest round barrow on the hills.

CHARGOT WOOD – Its name suggests that wild goats once lived here in this beautiful Forestry Commission woodland. There is a lovely round walk taking in some glorious views. There is also a 2¹/₂ mile walk to Luxborough, where one can enjoy a break in the Royal Oak Inn before returning.

Beverton Pond: source of the River Tone.

KENNISHAM WOOD – This wood can easily be explored using the Forestry Commission footpaths. The trees were severely damaged in the gales of January 1976 and in January 1990. Newly planted trees are now growing, but complete replanting takes time.

GUPWORTHY – As one travels along the Wheddon Cross road from Beulah Chapel there is soon a signpost on the left hand side, marked Gupworthy Ford and Blagdon. Along this very narrow lane are the remains of a terminus of the Mineral Railway line. All that can be seen now is the hollowed out canyon where the railway used to run and turn around to start its journey back to Watchet.

Gupworthy was a thriving nineteenth-century industrial village with 100 inhabitants.

BEVERTON POND – Returning to the Y junction and Beulah Chapel, take the Bampton Road where lovely beech-lined hedges form a green tunnel. On the right hand side is Beverton Pond, which holds the spring and the source of the River Tone. On the opposite side of the road and about 50 yards further on, by a radio mast, is a bridle path which follows the line of the Tone down the valley to Clatworthy Reservoir. The Tone runs into the reservoir. The area above the dam is known as Kings Brompton Common.

MIDDLETON COURT – This estate is mainly forest and is now privately let to the Theed Forestry Estates.

WITHIEL FLOREY – Another manor held by the de Flory or de Fluri family. It is known that they were there from the year AD 1212.

Miners lived and lodged in this village whilst working in the mines at Ralegh's Cross and Luxborough.

The stream is called the Bessom and just before it flows into Wimbleball Lake there is a new road bridge called 'Bessom Bridge'.

ST MARY'S – The west tower still bears remains of the thirteenth century but this church has been restored. However there is still no electricity and the building is lit by oil lamps. It has a wonderful feeling of remoteness, set as it is on this hilltop. I read the visitors' book and smiled at an entry by a visitor from Alicante:

'A very good area for churches and for all the Nuns in Spain.'

BITTESCOMBE HILL – This hamlet is in the parish of Upton. The manor was once in the hands of the Bratton family. By 1883 the resident of the Manor was Lt Col. Ferguson-Davie J.P. who was then one of the chief landowners.

HADDON HILL – There are lovely views from the hill and many walks down to Wimbleball Lake, Bury, Upton and Hartford. It is real moorland and in spring the hill is golden with gorse, while summer brings the purple heather. Whortleberries can be seen for most of the year and in November to February the brown bracken and the swirling mist can, with imagination, appear more like Dracula country.

Whortleberries grow in the acid soil, but also like a fair amount of peat and a good rainfall. They belong to the same family as the American cultivated blueberries.

When the American soldiers left the area at the end of the Second World War they buried food and equipment on Haddon Hill to save carrying it home. Occasionally tins of chicken or similar food have been unearthed.

RADDINGTON – This is a scattered village which lies around the hillside. At the time of Domesday it was in the hands of Roger Arundel. Chubworthy Farm is reputed to be eleventh century, Upcott Farm twelfth century, and Batscombe and Nutwell Farms both fifteenth century. Oxenlease Farm is a caravan and camping site and a good place to stay for coarse fishing.

There used to be a mill here on the stream which eventually empties into the Batherm.

The parish 'living' was a rectory from 1262 until 1927 when it was united with Chipstable. Since 1971 Raddington has been officially a chapelry within a parish.

A poor house was established here by John Kemp and an unknown benefactor. Additions were made by William Yeandle of Upton in 1754 and by George Davys in 1786. The tomb of the founder is in the churchyard.

The poor house was situated on a plot in the north-east corner from the church and within living memory it had a thatched roof.

Shute Hill means 'water shooting down the hill' and there are a lot of springs and water around this area.

ST MICHAEL'S CHURCH – It is quite a surprise to find on a field gate the sign 'St Michael's Church'. A walk across this field takes one to the churchyard gate. The church, which hasn't changed much since the day it was built, is very small and attractive.

The tower is thirteenth century but was restored in 1675; the date is on the side.

St Michael was the angel who threw the Devil out of heaven and so most sites of St Michael are probably pagan and have had churches on them from that time. It is thought that there has been a church there at least from King Alfred's time.

There is still part of what was an old water stoup in the porch, an indication of the church's age; water stoups were only to be found in porches until medieval times.

In the chancel is a very old memorial, difficult to read, to a former Mayor of Tiverton, Devon. There is also a commemoration dated 1852 of Thomas Davys, who was a church warden and probably a relation of George Davys, mentioned above.

SKILGATE – Yet another manor held by Roger Arundel; before the Conquest it was kept by Goda from Norway. The village lies on the south side of the Brendon Hills. The common land in Skilgate was enclosed in 1804 following the legal enclosure of common land.

Mrs Martin said her grandfather, who was a tailor in Skilgate before the turn of the century, used to go up to Ralegh's Cross for a drink. One night there was a fight between two of the miners and one was killed. The surviving miner was helped by his friends and they buried the victim in one of the hedges near the pub. He was assumed missing and as far as she knows he has never been found to this day.

Mrs Martin's father used to haul stone by horse and cart from a quarry in Upton for the building of the Upton Parsonage.

At this time the Post Office and the baker's shop used to be one and the same. The village also had a cooper, a cobbler and a stone mason all now sadly gone.

UPTON – This village sits below Haddon Hill and actually lies in the Haddon Valley, but is nevertheless 1000 feet above sea level. It is well scattered and consists for the greater part of farms which form many hamlets such as Rainsbury, Beechcombe, Bittescombe and Lowtrow Cross. There are two separate streams which run through the parish, one on each side, then both drain into the Wimbleball Lake. One of them is the River Haddeo and over it is a very small ancient clapper bridge, similar in design to the larger clapper bridge at Tarr Steps.

By 1791 the manor was in the hands of Sir Thomas Dyke Acland.

Through the Enclosure Acts the common land here was enclosed in 1804.

There is mention in 1861 of Lady Harriet's Drive, a very picturesque drive leading all the way from Bury.

By 1861 there was an infants' school. A new school was erected in 1876, given by the Ferguson-Davie family of Bittescombe Manor. It was closed in the mid 1970s. The building was then used as a Field Study Centre for school children from other parts of the country. This eventually also closed down and reverted to the Ferguson-Davie Estate. It has now been converted and sold as a private residence.

There was a chapel for Bible Christians, converted to the United Methodists when rebuilt in 1878.

Cranmer House was the parsonage built in 1905. A plaque in the oratory of this house reads:

> THIS PARSONAGE WAS BUILT IN 1905
> AND
> THE ENDOWMENT OF THE LIVING AUGMENTED BY
> NOBLETT HENRY CRANMER RODDOCK D.D J.P.
> OF VENNE HOUSE IN THE PARISH.
> BORN 22ND MAY 1851 – DIED 6TH JAN 1918.
> SUSTINUIT EI NOS JUSTINEBIT DEUS.

In 1910 the house and land were conveyed to the Diocese of Bath and Wells. The Rector of Upton presumably lived in the house from that date but there is no documentary evidence to hand. In 1932 the Governors of the Bounty of Queen Anne gave the house and Glebe land (10,200 square yards) free of charge to the Ecclesiastical Commissioners to use as a residence for the incumbents of the united benefice of Upton and Skilgate. In 1970 the benefice of Upton and Skilgate was united with that of Brompton Regis and Withiel Florey and the Rev. Michael Stagg became the first vicar of the united benefices. The rectory was sold in 1970 as a private house. The new owners were prohibited under the covenants of sale from calling it 'The Old Rectory' or 'Old Parsonage' and so they chose, with suitable connotations, the name 'Cranmer' – one of the names of the builder and of course derived from the Archbishop Cranmer who served in this area.

ST JAMES' CHURCH – The tithes of Upton belonged to St Nicholas Priory, Barlynch. The church was situated on a remote hillside and by 1872 it had ceased to be used and rapidly fell into disrepair. A new church was erected in 1867 at the side of the road in the hamlet of Rainsbury. The cost of £1,297.12s.6d. was raised by public subscription and by the kindness of Col. Ferguson-Davie J.P. who was one of the chief donors. The three old bells dated 1450, 1540 and 1609, which were in the tower of the old church were moved there where they rest. There is only one bell hanging in the new church; it is in the chancel arch. Of the old fourteenth-century church of St James only the tower remains.

ST JAMES' TOWER – This crumbling tower stands in a field of Upton Farm, now Rainsbury Farm, surrounded by tombstones in what was once its churchyard. All that remains adjoining the tower is the outline of what was once the nave.

During 1973, and after a century of neglect, the remains of the church passed to the Redundant Churches Fund who had the tower repaired, and now sometimes a midsummer open-air service is held at the Church.

MOREBATH – A very small village which once used to be called Morbach (in 1558) and Moorbade (by the seventeenth century). The word signifies the bath or pool in the manor. There are many warm springs around the village. A cattle fair was held there every August. In 1688 John Brook founded and endowed almshouses for two people. According to the Directory in 1881 there were 430 inhabitants.

During the Second World War the Royal Observer Corps were trained in aircraft recognition and had a look-out post in a field above the road between Morebath and Bampton; from there they could report aircraft sightings.

Trains used to run through Morebath Junction from Taunton to Dulverton and from Exeter to Dulverton. The line was abandoned in 1963 under Doctor Beeching's sweeping review. At Lodfin Cross just outside the village, the path of the Exe Valley railway line from Exeter to Dulverton can still be seen. Crossing gates were operated there by the keeper who lived in the adjacent Keeper's Cottage, which is now called 'Primrose Cottage'.

In the fields by the crossing towards Bampton three bombs were dropped, unloaded by a damaged German plane.

A lovely array of wild orchids at Coldharbour Farm reminded me of why there are dark spots on the leaves of orchids. Many of them grew around the cross on Calvary and drops of Jesus's blood fell onto the leaves.

ST GEORGE'S CHURCH – The first vicar was Ralph Turberville, 1259-1265. The church was restored in 1874 by voluntary subscriptions. It has a beautiful black marble Victorian font. The records kept by the rectors at the time of the Dissolution and the Reformation are still there. They were probably hidden in someone's house at the time.

BROMPTON REGIS – This is a quaint little village, also sometimes called Kings Brompton. One of the first things I noticed was a very large Chile Pine (Monkey Puzzle Tree), quite unusual in these little combes and hills. The trees were a novelty imported from South America just over a hundred years ago.

The village is divided into Higher Town and Lower Town. The church and the pub are in Higher Town, and next door to each other (Heaven and Hell!). All the houses and the very few shops are well kept. The George Inn was named after King George I, with excellent food and animals to amuse.

In Lower Town there is an interesting craft shop.

Before the Battle of Hastings in 1066 the parish was known as the King's Manor of Brunstone, and held by Harold's mother Ghida. Even after the Conquest Ghida lived there until after King William's death.

The village was a market town in the Hundred of Williton. It was granted the right to hold a fair on The Feast of the Assumption of Our Lady which is on 15 August. Later it was allowed to hold two fairs a year and a weekly market.

Brompton Regis Common was enclosed in 1804 under the Enclosure Act.

In 1878 there was a wagon works and a building yard. Two men worked for four shillings a day (20p). The wages for the month of February came to a grand total of £2. 12s. 0d. Most bills were charged annually after people had sold their animals at the Kings Brompton Fair. The village shop then offered free meat and pickles to all who paid their bills.

ST MARY THE VIRGIN CHURCH – There is a rood staircase but many churches in Victorian times (restoration was in 1853) were restored with very little care or thought for the past. The first clergyman recorded was William de Hawkedon in 1270, but it is known that there was a church on the site before that, probably Saxon.

There is a lovely old chest dated 1630-40. It was nearly destroyed by bonfire in the 1890s. It was rescued by the Ridler family and in 1988 was restored to its present state by Mr J. Ridler and given back to the church.

One of the bells in the church came from Barlynch Priory.

BARLYNCH PRIORY – In the reign of King Henry II (1154-89), the Royal Manor passed into the hands of William de Say. He founded a small priory of Augustinian Canons, dedicated to St Nicholas at Barlynch, on the edge of the parish. This was closed by Henry VIII on the Dissolution in 1537. It was demolished and some of the stones used to build a farmstead and a cottage. The lead from the roof and windows – 13 tons in all – was sent to Bristol for the King. The ruins of Barlynch Priory lie in the Exe Valley north of Dulverton. The Priory was endowed with the Manor and Church of Brompton Regis.

BARLYNCH ANIMAL SANCTUARY – Just along the road from Brompton Regis is the Animal Sanctuary, which is also the home of the League Against Cruel Sports. The 87-acre sanctuary was bought by Beatle, Paul McCartney for more than £100,000 in 1991.

LOUISA GATE – Opposite the animal sanctuary is the start of a beautiful forest walk. It is well marked by yellow signs on the trees and one can walk to Hartford, Bury or Wimbleball, all fairly short distances. A strange thing happened to me while walking the footpath to Bury; my dog suddenly ran off chasing a large black animal, much too big for a cat and certainly a much faster animal than the dog who came back exhausted. I believe I witnessed the Beast of Exmoor!

In those woodlands there is also quite a fair habitation of grey squirrels. Towards the end of the nineteenth century the red squirrel population had reached record numbers; 2000 were shot in one year alone in the New Forest. In 1876 a Mr Brocklehurst released a pair of North American grey squirrels into Henbury Park, Chelsea, which eventually saw the decline of the red squirrel. The grey squirrel is a much more aggressive creature, and also the red squirrel is more susceptible to disease. Another major cause of its decline was the destruction of its woodland habitat during the Second World War.

WIMBLEBALL LAKE – Early in 1965 the River Exe Joint Advisory Committee, made up of the West Somerset, North Devon and East Devon Water Boards, and the Devon River Authority, invited a firm of consulting engineers to prepare a report on the water resources of the River Exe and to consider potential reservoir sites. Of 17 likely places Wimbleball set across the River Haddeo was chosen. In 1974 work started on this

Dam at Wimbleball Lake, holding back nearly five million pre-metrication gallons of water.

reservoir. It was completed in 1978 at a cost of £11 million. It holds 4743 million gallons of water. The dam itself is 164 feet high. Willow and alder trees were planted around the edges of the lake. The wonderful cries of the Canada, Barnacle and Emperor Geese, who all breed on the water, can be heard. The reservoir is also used as a leisure lake for boating or fishing. Fishing permits can be obtained at the nearby Hill Farm. There is a nature trail around the banks of the water, a walk of about 8 miles. The reserve around Wimbleball was set up in 1978 and it includes woodland, scrub, marshland, grassland and a reed bed. West Hill Wood and Wimbleball Wood are ancient indigenous woodlands growing sessile oak and birch.

BURY – This pretty little hamlet lies in the Haddeo Valley. There was a dye house here at the height of the wool industry; children used to collect certain plants to make the dyes. People started growing and cultivating the most commonly used dyes in their gardens.

After crossing the deep ford in the centre of the hamlet or the ancient bridge, which is too narrow for vehicles, one immediately comes to a fork in the road and faces a disused chapel. This was first a school, then an Anglican chapel and is now a private residence. On the right is a 'No Through Road', which soon forks into two footpaths. The path to the left is a steep path up through the woodland, called the 'mile long hill', which comes out at Louisa Gate. The bridle path on the right is called 'Lady Harriet's Drive'. It once belonged to the Acland family. Lady Harriet Fox-Strangways married John Acland of Pixton. In 1777 Major Acland was injured when forming the advance guard of General Fraser's brigade in the American War of Independence and was captured and taken prisoner. Lady Harriet obtained permission to see her husband and under a flag of truce she crossed the enemy lines and nursed her husband back to health. On November 11th, 1778 Major Acland fought a duel on Bampton Down and four days later was dead. In 1785 Lady Harriet lost her young son, also called John.

Lady Harriet ordered the construction of a road through the beautiful woodlands of the Haddeo Valley in about 1805, to make the access easier from the Pixton estate to Wiveliscombe.

BURY CASTLE – The River Haddeo flows from Wimbleball and into the River Barle. At the confluence of those two rivers sits Bury Castle. It can be found on the Minehead to Bampton road. The name Bury means 'fortified place'. The circular castle was a motte and bailey castle erected by the Normans on the site of an old Iron Age fort. It is about 100 yards in diameter and the ditch is about 20 feet deep. It is not to be confused with the other Bury Castle, which lies on Exmoor near Selworthy.

HARTFORD – On walking Lady Harriet's Drive from Bury, one soon comes to the hamlet of Hartford. There is a trout hatchery and there was once a ford, as the name suggests. The footpath now crosses a private, well kept lawn. After that there is a field and then a cattle grid, which leads on to a track and under the forbidding walls of the dam. On the gate by the cattle grid a notice warns: 'Horse Riders please beware, there is a Stallion running with the Exmoor Ponies'. Carry on up this lane, past the dam and half a mile further on is the car-park for Wimbleball and some public toilets.

EXTON – This is another old Domesday settlement once known as Essetone. A very steep hill leads one down into this little village perched on the side of the hill; an even steeper hill continues down to Bridgetown with its shop and Post Office. The village is largely untouched by tourists because of its hill and inaccessibility.

The first building of note is the Exton Hotel. Opposite, the Old School House and the Old School are both now residential. There was a public house until the 1930s, called the Hare and Hounds; it is still marked. Until that time the main mode of transport in the area was the horse, but the hill which we came down was far too steep for horses. The original road ran diagonally across the hill passing by the church, crossing the road and continuing into the farm next door to the hotel. Stone Cottages were erected in 1890.

ST PETER'S CHURCH – Norman traces can be found in this small church, known as the 'rudest and roughest of its kind in the district'. When the church was restored in 1976, medieval tiles were found under the altar floor. They now form a step in the chancel. There is a peal of six bells, the oldest being from the sixteenth century and cast by Roger Sempson, mentioned earlier. One should look at this church, if only for the views and, as the church guide says, when leaving may God's Blessing go with you.

HEATHPOULT CROSS – Black grouse lived on the commons in the area for hundreds of years, but their numbers have diminished owing mainly to intensive farming. The birds need lots of space and live basically on heather and whortleberries. Their nests are always built of dead grass, lined with feathers and situated on the ground in the long heather. The pale yellow eggs spotted with dark brown blotches usually number between seven and eleven. Some say Heathpoult Cross was named to commemorate them, heath because it was heathland and poult for poultry, although this is debatable as there was a Lord Heathpoult.

A crossroads has been there for many centuries. It was the old coach road to Minehead and it was there that it once crossed the Harepath (Herpath), an ancient Saxon trackway across the Brendons.

At the time of the mining industry there was an inn at Heathpoult Cross, run by the Pope family (see Wheddon Cross), but it is no longer there.

LYPE HILL – This is the highest point on the Brendon Hills at 1400 feet above sea level.

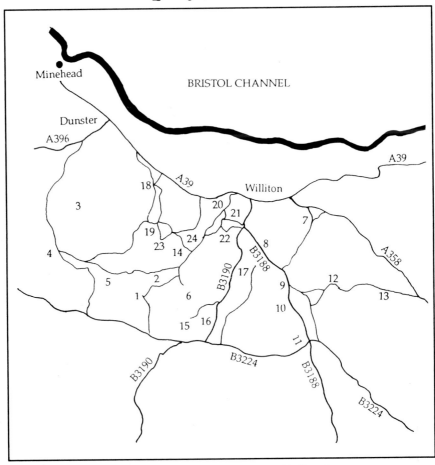

1. Treborough
2. Treborough Woods Nature Reserve
3. Croydon Woods
4. Luxborough
5. Pooltown
6. Leighland
7. Sampford Brett
8. Woodford
9. Monksilver
10. Combe Sydenham
11. Elworthy
12. Stogumber
13. Heddon Oak
14. Roadwater
15. Comberow
16. Timwood
17. Nettlecombe Court
18. Withycombe
19. Rodhuish
20. Hungerford
21. Torre
22. Beggearn Huish
23. Felons Oak
24. Golsoncott

TREBOROUGH – This means the place of the waterfall. There is a Bronze Age barrow on Treborough Common and it is known that the Romans had a settlement there as Roman tools and remains have been found.

The Manor was once held by the Saxon Edric, who was replaced by Ralph of Limsey at the Conquest.

Treborough was once the heart of the iron mining and slate quarrying community. By 1866 the quarries were in full production and Treborough was a much larger village than it is today. The slate quarry produced some of the finest blue slate, and in the nineteenth century wealthier people started having their roofs covered in Treborough slate instead of thatch.

By 1861 there was a small parochial school for children of both sexes. A board of five members was formed on January 12th 1881 and the parochial school was replaced by the Board School which was erected in 1865 with a separate residence for the school mistress.

Travelling along the road from Treborough to Roadwater just past the triangle of grass, park the car near the gateway to the council dump on the right. On the opposite side of the road are yellow footpath markers which lead to a nature trail in Langridge Wood, where there is much evidence of the old slate workings.

Further down the road towards Roadwater, on the right hand side in the wooded area, are several disused lime kilns.

ST PETER'S CHURCH – The Church of St Peter is thirteenth century, although there was a church on the site previously. The first vicar noted is in 1322.

In the churchyard there are two gravestones side by side. The first is of Isaac Chedzoy who met his death at the Treborough slate quarry on 8 December 1875, aged forty-five years. The stone beside it is of Isaac Chedzoy who met his death by an accident on December 8 1875, aged forty-five years. Were there two Isaac Chedzoys, of the same age in the same village, killed by an accident on the same day or does one man have two gravestones?

The medieval stone cross still stands. Such crosses were a prominent feature of villages in bygone years. The Treborough cross is not entirely the original and the church guide states that a new shaft was put on between 1830 and 1877.

A small slate-lined grave was uncovered under a small round barrow in Langridge Wood in 1820. The barrow dated from between 1500 BC and 2000 BC. The prehistoric female skeleton which it contained was re-interred in the corner of the churchyard, but unfortunately I couldn't find any grave or marker to confirm that.

TREBOROUGH WOODS NATURE RESERVE – This is an old oak coppice and mixed wood-land. Scrub is gradually colonising the spoil heaps from the slate quarries on the hillside above. Slate was quarried here from medieval times until 1938.

CROYDON WOODS – These woods, by the Dunster to Luxborough road, can easily be explored by way of Forestry Commission footpaths and beautiful views can be admired from high points, the highest being 1197 feet. There is a picnic area.

I have another true story to relate regarding these woods. A friend of my daughter's believed he saw the Beast of Exmoor in Croydon Wood. It was Christmas Eve and four lads decided to park the car and walk a little of the trail. One of them suddenly turned around and found they were being stalked by a big black creature. It ran off when they all turned to look. A few months later he told another friend about this and they decided to try to find it. They armed themselves with tins of Kit-e-Kat and when they got to the forest emptied the cat food out on a stone, put the tins back in the car and sat and waited for the Beast to appear. Of course it didn't show up. Eventually they gave up and drove back to Taunton. Going along Wellington Road they were exceeding the speed limit and were stopped by police. When they wound down the window and the policeman put his head in the car he met a terrible smell. He probably didn't know what it was and thought immediately of drugs or such.

'Where have you been and what have you been doing?' he asked.

'Well, actually officer we have been feeding the Beast of Exmoor,' they replied.

'Don't try to be funny with me son,' replied the officer.

The young men's sighting of the beast is recorded in the list of Beast sightings. I never reported my sighting at Louisa Gate.

LUXBOROUGH – Luxborough is another one of the highest points in the Brendons and yet Kingsbridge, the centre of the village, stands less than 600 feet. There is evidence of prehistoric settlements. The village was mentioned in Domesday and at that time was known as Lolchesberie.

In December 1837 nature turned upside down. Birds sang as in the summer, strawberries were picked, roses were in bloom and a chasm about 16 feet wide and four feet deep split the hillside and water gushed out of Colley Hill. There are lots of springs in the area and the River Washford rises near the village.

The village looks down the valley towards Druids Combe in the east. A lovely old inn called The Royal Oak serves delicious food. There is a walk through the woodland to the picnic site at Croydon Hill, and another footpath (mentioned earlier under Dunster) leads to Dunster and Timberscombe. The footpath south leads to Chargot Wood and about a mile to the west of this can be found Kennisham picnic site.

The Forestry Commission own Slowley Wood where a walk has magnificent views across the Channel to Wales.

ST MARY'S CHURCH – The tower is early fourteenth century. There is a beautiful stained glass east window to the memory of Bertram Escott Lethbridge who died age twenty-one from wounds at Ladysmith in South Africa. Dated 1899, it is the only stained glass window in the church. There was most certainly a church on this site before the Conquest. The lands belonged to the de Mohuns at Dunster who gave the

Luxborough Church: one of the highest points in the Brendons.

living to the Priory at Bruton. The whole church – pews, pulpit and windows – is very plain. In the churchyard are the stump of the ancient village cross and an old plough. During the Middle Ages the communal plough was always kept in the church.

POOLTOWN – This is a hamlet belonging to Luxborough. In 1280 the manor was held by one Hugo de la Pole, which is how it acquired its name.

LEIGHLAND – At the time of Domesday the King held Cleeve of which this was part. There was a school in this village attended by over 100 children at the beginning of the century. With the decline of the mining industry it eventually had to close. It was situated next to the chapel and it is now a private residence. There also used to be shops in two of the cottages.

ST GILES' CHAPEL – There has probably been a place of worship on this site since Saxon times. This building is named after a medieval chapel which served the nearby Cleeve Abbey. The monks erected the first chapel there and luckily it survived the Dissolution of the Monasteries. The chapel was served by the monks until 1320 when they were forbidden to act as parish priests. In May 1320 a vicarage was constituted by the Bishop of Bath and Wells.

In 1611 Robert Poyntz left money in his will for the future maintenance of the chapel. During the days of the miners, when the population increased, Leighland became a separate parish. The chapel was completely rebuilt in 1862 to accommodate the growing community.

After the decline in the mining industry the parish again became united with Old Cleeve in 1955.

SAMPFORD BRETT – This pretty village appears as one long street with the church as the backcloth at the end. A little stream trickles down on one side and the old school building is at the end opposite the church.

Sir Reginald Fitzurse lived near Sampford Brett. He was the leader of the knights who killed Thomas à Becket and was an ancestor of Florence Wyndham.

The Manor in Saxon times belonged to Alwyn and at the Conquest it was given to Roger de Courcelles, a relative of King William. Later the line came down to Margaret who married a de Brito. She bore a son who in turn had five sons, one of whom was Richard de Brito, also one of the four knights responsible for the death of Thomas à Becket.

Richard's brother Simon became Lord of the Manor of Sandford and Torweston and later Simon's son John inherited the Manor. By that time the name had become de Brett, hence the village name. Simon died in 1225 and was buried in the church. His son Willam has an effigy tomb in the vestry. Wiliam was once the Coroner of Somerset; he died in 1295.

In 1306, Sir Adam de Brett was granted a Royal Charter to hold a weekly market and an annual fair at Sampford Brett.

In 1359 the de Bretts were prevailed upon to hand over their properties to the de Courtenay family; it remained with the de Courtenays for over four centuries.

There are the remains of an old lime kiln at Lime Ridge.

In the Middle Ages church wardens and overseers of the poor collected money from the rich to pay for the needs of the poor. The following relating to the year 1694 comes from *St George's Church Guide*.

The Poor Tax of £2. 9s. 9d. was collected seven times during 1694. Collections depended on the need. The same procedure took place in every village and town.

How the money was spent in 1694

	£	s	d
Expenses when Overseer took office		4	10
To ? from 3/4/93 to 10/4/94.	3	19	0
Paid for the keeping of Grace Risdon for 51 weeks	2	11	0
To Joan Isott 20 Nov at 9d. 31 weeks at 12d. to April llth	2	6	0
Paid Widow Lafkins 13 weeks at 12d. and 12 weeks at 8d.	1	11	0
Paid Mr Glass for Feoffment deed		10	0
Paid Thomasine Amory several times in his infirmity		10	6
To William Binding several times in his sickness		5	6
For a shroud for Thomas Lafkins		5	0
To Robert Binding several times in his infirmity		5	6
To James Binding and his wife in their sickness		5	6
To Will Long for mending Grace Risdon's shoes several times		1	6
To him for mending Joan Isott's shoes			9
To him for mending two pairs of shoes for Joan Isott		5	0
To Thomas Towell for extra Ordinary charges towards the Highways		7	6
To William Lulby and ? for amending the Highways	1	15	0
To Thomas Lafkin at several times in his sickness		5	6
For a warrant to send away John Stallonge		1	0
For a cappe for Grace Risdon		1	3¹/₂
For an order to remove John Stallonge		2	6
For a bodice for Joan Isott		1	10
For Stockings for Joan Isott and Grace Risdon		1	8
For a warrant for ?		1	0
For John Cross for riting to the Clock			6
For an order for a Way Warden		2	6
For a paid of bodices for Grace Risdon		2	4
For a change and a skirt for Grace Risdon and for making		7	7
For two aprons and a cloth for Joan Isott		2	8
For our expenses at Watchet		2	0
Laid out for Widow Long		3	0
For a coat and waistcoat for Joan Isott and a coat for Thomas Larkins wife	1	2	4
For a trunk to keep the writings		3	4
Paid the way wardens		1	6
For keeping our accounts		3	0

St George's Church – A church was built here in the early 1300s but there was probably a church on the site before that. It is thought possibly that the church was built by the de Britos in atonement for the death of Thomas à Becket. The tower was built in 1360. An extensive restoration was carried out between 1830 and 1840 and even the shape of the church changed. That was when the effigy of William de Brett was moved from the north transept and placed in the vestry.

Simon Warman's (Werman) carved bench ends are in the church. Warman's trade mark is the edging, consisting of a long stem crossed at intervals by an oak leaf. Just inside the church on the left is a bench end of Florence Wyndham, with twins she bore after returning from the dead.

During the restoration the old stone font was taken to Williton workhouse to baptise the babies of paupers and was replaced by a black marble one. When the workhouse closed and became a geriatric hospital unit the stone font was once more returned to its original position.

The fifteenth-century bosses were cleaned in 1951 and are well worth seeing.

WOODFORD — Here a blade mill once sharpened all the tools of the area. This is now a private residence.

In 1773 a ghastly murder took place. Three women, Elizabeth Conibeer, aged eighty-eight, and her two daughters, Anne forty-five, and Sarah forty-three, were in their kitchen with money on the table waiting for the baker to collect. Someone came and axed the three women to death. When the baker arrived he found the three ladies lying in a great pool of blood and his money was on the table as usual. The baker was so upset he was never the same man again. The murderer was never found; the motive was clearly not robbery. The women's bodies were buried in Monksilver churchyard.

There was a poorhouse in the hamlet by 1870.

MONKSILVER — Until 1066 this manor was held by Edward the Confessor. After the Conquest it passed to Roger of Courseulles and Alfred of Spain; the latter had to pay dues of 18 sheep per year.

Monksilver is a pretty little winding village with thatched and colour washed cottages. Monk is obvious but Silver comes from the Latin 'Silva' which means a wooded area, the Monks' Wood. The Ram Inn was established by 1675, and had changed its name to the Half Moon by 1785. A cottage still bears the name. Since the 1860s the village pub has been The Notley Arms. Its name derives from the Notley family who followed the Sydenham family at Combe Sydenham, about a mile away.

There is a lovely walk south westward through woodlands below Bird Hill and on towards Sticklepath. Until the nineteenth century there were several cottages along the lane to Bird Hill. There is a walk at the top of Bird Hill. Follow the 'No Through Road' through Colton Farm and on to Holcombe Water, where three streams meet. Cross the little wooden bridge and follow the path through the woodland of Galloping Bottom to Holcombe Water Farm.

There was a quarry in the parish prior to 1841 and copper is thought to have been mined at Beech Tree Cross.

The main road through the valley was turnpiked in 1765.

ALL SAINTS' CHURCH — The church is fifteenth century and built of red sandstone. It has a wagon roof.

Look in the head of one of the windows in the aisle, where there can clearly be found a hammer, nail, pincers, a horseshoe and a buttress. The story goes that the local blacksmith ordered a hundredweight of iron from Bristol and when the consignment arrived he discovered that it was gold. He considered that mistake gave him the right to own it, and with the money from his good fortune he built the church aisle leaving the implements of his trade in the window for all to see.

In the churchyard is the grave of Elizabeth Conibeer and her two daughters, who were victims of the murder at Woodford. The tombstone (which I couldn't find) is said to read as follows:

> In memory of Elizabeth Conibeer aged Eighty Eight years.
> And her two daughters Anne Aged Forty Five and Sarah Forty
> Three who was all inhumanly Murdered in the day of the 5th
> June 1775 in their house in Woodford in this Parish.

There are also many graves bearing the name Notley, and relatives still live in the area.

COMBE SYDENHAM – This house lies deep in one of Exmoor's hidden valleys. The estate first came into the hands of the Sydenhams, and thus acquired its name, when Edward Sydenham of Bathealton married Joan, daughter and heir of Walter Combe, in 1482.

The Manor was sold again to the Rev. George Notley in 1800.

This house was completely rebuilt in the reign of Elizabeth I. Elizabeth Sydenham was a Maid of Honour to Queen Elizabeth, which is how she met Sir Francis Drake. The Sydenhams, however, did not want Sir Francis to marry Elizabeth, in spite of the fact that he was rich, famous and knighted, as he was only a commoner, the son of a yeoman farmer, and an old man. His first wife, Mary, died just three months after he bought Buckland Abbey. Elizabeth's father, George, wanted her married off to a rich young suitor and therefore wouldn't let her wait for Drake, who was away at sea serving the Queen. The wedding was arranged and as the bridal party arrived at the church door a canonball,

The pond and house, Combe Sydenham.

thought to have been fired by Drake, fell among the guests. That was thought to be an omen and the wedding did not take place. When Drake returned from sea he married Elizabeth, and the Sydenhams persuaded him to put all his money in the manors of Yarcombe, Sherford and Sampford Spiney set aside for the use of his wife and their heirs, but as with Drake's first marriage there were no children. It was a very shrewd move on the part of the Sydenhams, as within a few years Drake was dead and their daughter, later the Countess of Devonshire, became one of the richest women alive. Drake died aboard his ship in 1596 from dysentery, which spread through all his crew.

The cannon ball which stopped a wedding, reputedly fired by Sir Francis Drake to frighten off a rival suitor for the hand of Elizabeth Sydenham.

The Elizabethan manor house of Combe Sydenham lies almost hidden. The present owners, Mr and Mrs William Theed, are restoring the house and it is open to the public. The canonball is reputedly a meteorite. It can be seen displayed on the flagstones in the Court Room and it is said to bring one luck if it is touched.

There is a nature walk through field and forest and one will almost certainly see fallow deer roaming in the deer park. Walled gardens, ornamental tree nurseries and a country trout farm are some of the attractions. An Elizabethan overshot water-powered mill has recently been restored and is grinding locally-grown hard wheat into stone-ground flour. A master baker is employed and bread can be bought there which contains only traditional natural ingredients. During the restoration of the mill, the 19-foot high wall and the leat had to be completely rebuilt.

The estate also produces fine timber. There is a useful 'educational forestry trail' with boxes set up in the woods containing stories and information about each tree.

The owners have now become the first people in Somerset to receive a Centre of Excellence award for the woodland and visitor centre.

ELWORTHY — The village of Elworthy lies on the eastern slopes of the Hills on the B3188 road from Monksilver. It was originally part of the Saxon minster belonging to Stogumber. Before the Conquest it was held by the Saxon Dunn but it was given to William de Mohun of Dunster by William the Conqueror. During Saxon times it was a place known for the breeding of eels, very valuable and desirable food. By 1253 it belonged to William Malet who gave it to the Order of St John of Jerusalem. By the seventeenth century one of the most prominent families were the Laceys from nearby Hartrow and that family filled many pews in the church.

Plash Farm is known to be at least seventeenth century.

Elworthy Cross House was a toll house belonging to the Wiveliscombe Turnpike Trust. The Wiveliscombe to Watchet road and the Bampton to Hartrow road were turnpiked in the late 1700s/early 1800s. 'Save a Penny Lane' was a lane running between Brompton

Ralph and Stogumber which skirted east of Elworthy and avoided the toll house.

Take the little lane beside the church and continue walking until the main road is reached, turn right and at the top of the hill enter the field on the left with the radio mast. There is a large earthwork or fort, called Elworthy Barrows. People lived there over 4000 years ago. The view here is amazing, many ranges of hills can be seen, including Dunkery Beacon. There is now a trig point and this is where the ancient trackway known as 'The Prayway' started, running on to Quarm and deeper into Exmoor at Exford and on into Devon. From the year 1556, if not earlier, two braziers stood here. Watchmen were stationed on site and they had to look towards Cleeve Hill above Watchet. When an enemy was expected they had to fire one of the beacons; they fired both beacons only if an invasion actually took place. There is a reproduction of a brazier at Ralegh's Cross Inn.

ST MARTIN'S CHURCH — This is a very small church, with a pulpit reached by a rood loft stairway. The rood screen was made in the nineteenth century but the frieze dates from 1632 and there is some fifteenth-century tracery. It bears the Lacey coat of arms and crest.

The font is carved out of alabaster collected from Blue Anchor in the seventeenth century.

The census of 1971 shows only 82 people residing in Elworthy and the maintenance of the church became impossible. It was declared redundant in 1979 and vested in the Redundant Churches Fund.

STOGUMBER — The village took its name from its first Norman Lord of the Manor, Stoke de Gomer. In the main street are the almshouses dating from the seventeenth century; records kept of the burials from these almshouses go back to 1668. They were donated by the Sydenhams and originally housed six poor old women who were given a shilling a week by the owners. The houses have now been bought privately and made into one large residence, The Almonry.

A phantom pack of hounds is alleged to run through the village to Wills Neck on the Quantocks on certain nights of the year.

Three local men were executed for supporting Monmouth (see Heddon Oak); after death their heads were boiled in salt water, then tarred and stuck on poles as a warning to all.

A survey was carried out in 1686 to find out how many beds and how much stabling was available for the military in Somerset. In Stogumber alone there were 29 beds for soldiers and 15 stables for their horses.

The local public house is the White Horse Inn, but there used to be several inns in the village.

Stogumber still has its station on the line of the West Somerset Railway.

Near the station is Bee World, where one can see bees working in the hives – honey is extracted and potted – and find out how wax products such as candles, hand creams, bees wax etc are made. There is a wildflower and pond walk, room for children to play and easy access for the disabled. All that is set out against the background of this beautiful countryside.

One of Joan of Arc's judges, Cardinal Beaufort, used to hunt in the area.

The White Horse Inn was once part of the large market house which served as the village collecting place for wool from the surrounding district when the wool trade was at its height. After the fleece had been purchased by various landlords it was distributed to the cottages of their employees where it was spun and woven: a classic 'cottage industry'.

On the outskirts of the village are the remains of an old lime kiln.

THE CHURCH OF OUR LADY ST MARY — The church on this site was burnt down some time in the fourteenth century and only the lower part of the tower and south porch bear any remains of it. There was probably an even older wooden church on the site.

In the rebuilt fourteenth century church one can find the effigy tomb of Sir George Sydenham which rests in the Sydenham Chapel. It is a reminder of feudalism, when the Lord of the Manor had his own private chapel. His two wives are lying one each side of him; at his feet are three babies with their nurse.

There is a fourteenth century stone pulpit, one of the only two stone pulpits in West Somerset, the other being at Cheddon Fitzpaine.

Outside there is a small triangular patch of grass where there are only three recent graves. It was once a mass grave for the victims of plague.

HEDDON OAK — A large old oak tree which once grew outside Stogumber was cut down in 1979. It was the hanging tree. Judge Jeffreys had six supporters of Monmouth hung there after a battle took place in the vicinity, three men from Stogumber (mentioned above) and three from Crowcombe. There is a story that on the night of 22 September, 1690 some travellers were passing by when several ghostly rebels appeared. Many people since have reported having a choking feeling on passing the spot.

Judge Jeffreys became notorious for the severity of his sentences on those supposed to have supported Monmouth in the Battle of Sedgemoor. He became known as the Hanging Judge, because at the Bloody Assize he sentenced 292 out of 300 people to death.

It is said that the Duke of Monmouth went to see a clairvoyant before he set sail from Holland. She told him to 'beware of the Rhyne', but he had never heard of a rhine and didn't know what she was talking about.

He lost the Battle of Sedgemoor at Bussex Rhyne.

ROADWATER — This is a long winding village in the parish of Old Cleeve that stretches through the valley. It came into the family of Romara. William de Romara was created Earl of Lincoln by King Stephen in 1141. Its most famous old house has wooden mullions in its windows and a plaque bearing the date 1700. The Washford River meanders down from Comberow where there are remains of the mineral railhead.

There was a mill, now a private residence.

A large Methodist chapel was built in 1907. St Luke's Mission Room, used by the miners, seats 180 persons. The Village Hall which holds 170 persons was given by Mr and Mrs F.Beckitt and opened in 1928. The same year a five-acre recreation field was given by Captain J.W.Bridges of Croydon Hall.

The public house is The Valiant Soldier. This was mentioned in records of 1770 and it could be even older. There was also a pub called The New Inn which was opened in 1809 and continued in business until the 1920s.

A ghostly funeral possession is said to be seen on the road between Roadwater and Golsoncott – probably the same story as at Blue Anchor.

MINERAL RAILWAY LINE — In 1855 Parliament authorised the building of a railway to carry iron ore from the Brendon Hills to Watchet and a line known as the West Somerset Mineral Railway was built. Iron ore mining had been going on in the area spasmodically since Roman times. In the seventeenth century the work was carried out by Germans who were specially brought over, but the industry really developed in 1852 when two

Remains of engine house and winding house, Comberow.

Welshmen from Ebbw Vale formed the Brendon Hills Iron Company. Miners came from all over the country and houses and chapels were built for them. Being chapel folk they were mainly teetotal and their social life revolved around the Temperance Society.

The idea was to ship the iron ore across the Bristol Channel to Wales. The railway was built and completed as far as Ralegh's Cross by 1859 and an extension to Gupworthy was added by 1864, linking the mines with Watchet harbour 1300 feet below the hills. The steep incline up to Brendon and Gupworthy was to be carried out by rope working on a pulley basis, the descending laden trucks pulling the empty ones back to the top. The line opened to passengers on 4 September 1865 and there were passenger stations at Watchet, Washford, Roadwater and Timwood/Comberow. On 10 May, 1879 the mines closed down when cheaper ore was imported; the employees had only one week's notice. The hill miners had little alternative employment, which caused much hardship. By the end of 1879 the mines were re-opened but never at the former level of activity. The railway passenger service closed in 1898. By the turn of the century the price of iron ore fell drastically and the villages became deserted. The railway track and many of the buildings fell into disuse. The industry re-started in 1907, but for only two years as it was by then unprofitable. The railway lines were actually taken up and used for munitions during the Great War.

THE MINERS' HEALTH SERVICE – The mining company employed two surgeons to look after the men; one lived at Brendon Hill, the other at Watchet. A doctor lived at Roadwater and a midwife at Brendon Hill. If the breadwinner fell ill the lack of income was a constant worry. To encourage people to prepare for such eventualities a penny bank was opened in

September 1860. In 1870 The Court of the Ancient Order of Foresters was formed and soon became established with over 100 members. The men paid four pence a month and when they became sick or injured they would receive ten shillings a week. In 1871 an accident fund was also set up; this paid twelve shillings a week to disabled members.

COMBEROW – An accident involving two locomotives occurred on the afternoon of Saturday 22 August 1857; an engine left Roadwater with a truck carrying about 30 labourers returning to Watchet. On reaching Washford, Henry Giles, the crossing keeper, held up his flag and stopped the train. He asked the driver to wait there as a coal train was expected shortly from Watchet. John James, the assistant engineer who was riding on the engine, wanted to go on as he was in a hurry to get home. Giles climbed onto the buffer beam and they set off again at about 20 miles an hour, blowing the whistle loudly. On rounding a curve at Kentsford they suddenly saw the coal train about 200 yards away but it was too late for either train to stop. Henry Giles was killed instantly. John James and another man riding in the engine died later of their injuries. Several passengers were also injured.

At Comberow there is an incline three-quarters of a mile long with a gradient of 1 in 4 (800 feet).

By 1877 over 52,000 tons of iron ore was being moved. The station itself was demolished in the 1930s and the stone was reused, but the station master's house still exists. There was a mine shaft near here which has now been filled in.

The Washford River rises near Comberow and flows north to the Bristol Channel.

TIMWOOD – Meaning timber wood, this hamlet was once a busy little hamlet adjacent to the Mineral Railway line.

NETTLECOMBE COURT – At the drive to Nettlecombe Court (a valley of nettles) the notice board on the left reads 'The Leonard Wills Field Centre Field Studies Council'. On the right is a small cemetery in a corner of a field. At one end are several graves to the Trevelyan family; one is a beautiful cross to an only daughter dated as recently as 1906-28. The graveyard is still used today.

By the lych-gate (dated 1922) is a grave to the Right Honourable Sir Arthur Channell, Member of the High Court of Justice, King's Bench Division, dated 1858-1928, and his wife Constance, who was the daughter of Walter Trevelyan, also a Barrister-at-Law.

Down the drive there are two columns, once supporting Trevelyan horses; these have been removed as they were in urgent need of repair but will be replaced some time in the future.

Entrance to Nettlecombe Court: the horse's head commemorates equine quick thinking said to have saved the life of an early Trevelyan.

Nettlecombe Court and Church: the Tudor manor house now houses a Field Studies Centre.

Nettlecombe Court, is a Tudor manor house erected in 1599 on the site of a previous house. Like many other buildings in the Brendons, it too is built of red sandstone. The previous house belonged to Earl Godwin but in the reign of Henry II it was granted to the Ralegh family. Simon Ralegh was the last of that family and his niece married John Trevelyan in 1453. The first Trevelyan was supposed to have lived on the legendary land of Lyonesse and when that sank below the water his horse saved him by swimming away. Now a recurring design in the house shows a horse's head rising out of the waves. The lost land of Lyonesse was a land of magic and King Arthur rested there between conquests. It was off the far western tip of Cornwall and one day it suffered a calamity and disappeared into the sea.

The house has a fine hall, with a minstrel's gallery. The Trevelyan men regularly held the office of Sheriff of Somerset until the end of the eighteenth century. John Trevelyan, who died in 1622, is recorded as growing ten varieties of apple in his orchards; they were looked after for him by a Mr Pace. Other fruits were also grown and Mr Pace had a pear and a fig tree named after him. The large estate also reared many animals – hogs, heifers, steers, colts and sheep.

When the Civil War came the Trevelyans were staunch Royalists. The Rector of the church was a Parliamentarian; he gathered together a band of like-thinking men and they tried to burn down the Court.

There are several windows blocked out to save money while the window tax was in operation.

The Court now belongs to the Field Studies Council. It is not open to the public but parties may view it by appointment. Near the house is the church and ancient graveyard.

The Trevelyans owned much of the Parish of Treborough, including the slate quarry. Nettlecombe also used to boast some of the largest oaks in England.

ST MARY'S CHURCH — The church on the estate dates from 1260. There is an effigy tomb of Simon Ralegh who has his legs crossed, an indication that he went to the Crusades. (See Ralegh's Cross). Next is the tomb of John Ralegh who lies with his wife. He died in 1387. He was known as the seven foot giant.

There is a table tomb with inscriptions to John Trevelyan, who was buried in the year of our Lord 1623 and of his wife, Urith, and several children.

There is also a very old chalice and paten. The floor is made up of old flagstones.

The east window was installed in memory of Sir Walter John Trevelyan, 1866-1931; it has a picture of the house and the church in it, and represents the four seasons and of course the Trevelyan horse is also there.

WITHYCOMBE — The village is named after the willows which grew near the village stream and which were made into withies. This quiet unspoilt village lies adjacent to the busy A39 road.

Sandhill Farm is supposed to be haunted by Joan Carne, who died on 12 October 1612 and was buried in Withycombe churchyard. There is a plaque to her memory to the left of the organ in the church. She was a witch who lived in Sandhill Farm during the Middle Ages and whom everyone feared. She killed three husbands, one of whom was a Wyndham. She was buried in an iron coffin but after the funeral, when mourners returned to Sandhill Farm, she was supposed to have been there frying eggs and bacon and then turned herself into a hare and ran away. One man nearly caught her, beating the hare over the head. The next day she returned with her head bandaged. She continued to haunt the house and so it was decided to exorcise her. The priest arrived with 'bell, book and candle', along with a large gathering of interested local people. The local priest himself was supposed to have certain powers. Unfortunately someone saw her and shouted 'there her be', and everyone ran away. They decided to have a second attempt at 'laying the ghost' and on that occasion seven parsons turned up. They waited for her in a passage and as she approached they threw silk threads around her and led her to Sandhill Pond where she was laid under the water. She can now only return to Sandhill Farm by one cockstride each year. It is said that Sandhill farmhouse will burn down when she finally reaches it.

Model of St Nicholas in Withycombe Church.

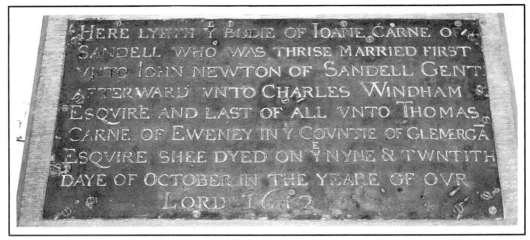

Plaque in St Nicholas' Church to Joan Carne,
witch of Sandhill Farm, which she is said to still haunt.

The pond to this day is called 'The Witch's Pool'.

When in 1883 Clement Kille, a journalist, visited The Witch's Pool, his dog gazed into the pond and pricked up its ears, then lifted up its foreleg as if in hunting mode. It then ran around the pond looking in it as if to get a better view of something. It had never done that before.

I met Mrs Hobbs, who lives at Sandhill Farm. She said that about six years ago they had a fire in one of the barns and everyone thought that the witch had returned, but it was in fact vandals who were caught and brought to justice.

Withycombe Common was in the hands of the Lord of the Manor and the medieval courts gave the commoners the right to graze their animals there. It now belongs to the Crown Estate.

Withycombe Scuffels is an area of semi-natural woodland, which had through the ages been worked on a twenty-four-year coppice rotation. It also belongs to the Crown Estate. The commoners were permitted to remove small branches of wood for fuel and repairs. It is well known for its flora and fauna, especially the lichens which show that this area is unpolluted. There are three circular walks of varying distances starting from Nutcombe Bottom car park.

ST NICHOLAS' CHURCH – This is a little white roughcast church dating from the thirteenth century and virtually unchanged; it seemed to have escaped the notice of the Victorians. There is a fourteenth century effigy of a woman in one wall and another of a man about the same date opposite. They both have hearts in their hands, which probably means that they died elsewhere and only their hearts were brought back here for burial. That was a common practice until the fifteenth century, as it was too expensive to carry bodies far. The man is wearing a hat, rare as the men's heads are usually bare. The lady is thought possibly to be Lucy de Meriet.

Also in the church is a colourful model of St Nicholas, the patron saint of children. The sculpture was made by Miss R.Reckitt of Golsoncott House, Golsoncott; she was over eighty when she finished it. She was also commissioned to make many inn signs. St. Nicholas was said to have saved three young girls from prostitution by anonymously paying their dowries with three bags of gold. The three bags of gold are portrayed at his feet.

RODHUISH – This little village with very winding roads is missed by the majority of tourists. The quaint church is dedicated to St Bartholomew. It has an old Norman font which was given to the parish by Carhampton in 1890.

Rodhuish Common is another area where the commoners had the right to graze their stock. The River Pill rises on Rodhuish Common.

HUNGERFORD – This small hamlet has Torre Fruit Farm where the owners make their own special cider, Torre Hatchery breeding fish, and the public house called The White Horse established in 1730. It was once a posting inn and the ostlers used to collect the horses and take them to the stables which are still there. There is also a mounting block still in position on the outside of the building. In the time of the turnpike trusts this was a collecting point for the Minehead United Trust until 1877.

TORRE – The mineral railway ran through Torre and on a corner of the road it can be clearly seen where the line ran across from one side of the road to the other.

BEGGEARN HUISH – There once was a very industrious quarry in this hamlet.

FELONS OAK – This oak tree was an ancient hanging tree. It has been cut down but the size of its trunk can still be seen. A new young oak tree has been planted alongside. The views from here over the Channel are excellent on a clear day. Croydon Hall School is also situated here. The Abbey Grange of Croydon was mentioned in the records of 1221.

GOLSONCOTT – This is another small hamlet and farming community in the parish of Old Cleeve, the meaning of which is golden sand and cottages.

Bibliography

My thanks go to the following:

The church magazine of Brompton Regis, Withiel Florey and Upton.

Somerset Legends, Berta Lawrence.

All the church and house guides.

Church and house information boards.

Exmoor National Park, Her Majesty's Stationery Office.

The History and Antiquities of Somerset, John Collinson.

Gerard's Particular Description of Somerset.

The Folklore of Somerset, Kingsley Palmer.

The Story of a Community and its Newspaper, Somerset County Gazette.

The Blackmore Country, Snell.

The Old Mineral Line, R.J.Sellick.

Victoria History of the County of Somerset, Vol.V.

Leland in Somerset, Bates.

Acknowledgements

I hope all the information is correct; I have tried to verify all of it. I thank all the numerous villagers who have given me their time, many of whom I can't name:

Capt T.Middleton and Lt. Richard Storrie and staff, Norton Manor Camp; Mrs Joan Lewis, Taunton; Brian Knight, Taunton; Mrs Hobbs, Sandhill Farm; Peter Andrews, Maundown; Dave Pursey, Clatworthy; Mr Heard, Bardon House; Mr Stowell, Old Cleeve; Mrs Martin, Taunton and Skilgate; Mrs Gauld, Upton; Dr Katherine Wyndham, Orchard Wyndham; Mr William Theed, Combe Sydenham; Capt. Jon Trouton, Wheddon Cross Farm; Mrs Mary White, Wheddon Cross; Alex Bowden, my daughter Dawn's friend; staff at the Cheese Factory, Tower Farms; Miss Rosemary Cox, Willett House; James Starkie, Gaulden Manor; Mr Webber, Cutcombe; Chris Young, Lydeard St Lawrence; Peter Boyce, Lydeard St Lawrence; Mrs Routley, Lydeard St Lawrence; Teresa Robb, Eastbourne; Mr Valentine and Mrs Jenny St John Webster, Ash Priors; Donald Gould, Bampton; Michael Rendell, Bampton; Mr A.Palmer, Milverton; the staff at the stations of Stogumber and Williton; David Bromwich, Local History Library, Taunton; Mrs D.James Taunton; Mrs Ann Taylor, Taunton Cider Company; staff, Watchet Market House Museum; Harold Inder; Colin Clements; the staff, The Breweries, Wiveliscombe; the owner, The Quaking House; Clara Sansom for cutting and editing; Stan Gwyther, friend and fellow author for proof reading this book; and my daughter, June Eckhart, for walking with me, and in whose company much of the information in the book was obtained.

Index